Preaching the Hard Words of Jesus

The Preacher's Toolbox

THE PREACHER'S TOOLBOX

COMMUNICATING GOD'S WORD WITH POWER

Preaching the Hard Words of Jesus

Steven D. Mathewson

Craig Brian Larson, General Editor

Preaching the Hard Words of Jesus

Hendrickson Publishers Marketing, LLC
P. O. Box 3473
Peabody, Massachusetts 01961-3473

ISBN 978-1-61970-101-4

Printed in the United States of America

First Hendrickson Edition Printing — July 2013

Library of Congress Cataloging-in-Publication Data

Mathewson, Steven D. (Steven Dale), 1961–
   Preaching the hard words of Jesus / Steven D. Mathewson.
      pages cm. — (The preacher's toolbox ; Book 6)
   ISBN 978-1-61970-101-4 (alk. paper)
      1. Jesus Christ—Teachings. 2. Preaching. 3. Bible. N.T. Gospels—
Homiletical use. I. Title.
   BS2415.M36 2013
   251—dc23
                              2013002409

Dedication

To Kevin Kneeshaw and Bob Schwahn,
friends who invited me often to share the gospel
with the Cru chapter at Montana State University
when the three of us all served in the Bozeman area.
They have encouraged me when I was down
and celebrated with me when I was up.
Their passion for sharing the gospel of Jesus Christ
continues to fuel my passion for proclaiming it.
They have sharpened me as iron sharpens iron,
and, yes, they have taught me
a bit about fly-fishing along the way!

CONTENTS

ACKNOWLEDGMENTS

More than fifty years ago, George Ladd suggested that Matthew 24:14 is the most important single verse in the Word of God for God's people today. This verse contains Jesus' words: "And this gospel of the kingdom will be preached in the whole world as a testimony to all nations, and then the end will come." What a privilege to write a couple of volumes which will, I pray, help pastors proclaim the gospel of the kingdom from the four Gospels.

First and foremost, I thank Brian Larson for inviting me to partner with PreachingToday.com and Hendrickson Publishers to help pastors overcome the challenges they face when preaching the four Gospels. Along the way, this project turned into *two* volumes! I am grateful for Brian's vision, support, and encouragement. It has been tremendous in every respect.

I am grateful to the gospel scholars who were willing to take time out of their busy schedules to help me think through many of the issues discussed in these volumes. I appreciate the breakfast and lunch meetings I had with Grant Osborne and Craig Blomberg. David Turner graciously took the time to interact with me extensively by e-mail on matters of Second Temple Judaism—the context in which the events in the four Gospels took place. D. A. Carson has kindly taken time over the past six years to meet me for breakfast and allow me to pick his brain on a variety of exegetical, theological, and pastoral issues. His love for the gospel inspires me.

The elders of the Evangelical Free Church of Libertyville (IL) have been very supportive of my writing ministry and have encouraged me to serve the wider church through it. Their influence has made me a better pastor and preacher. So I offer my thanks to Bryan Cope, Tom Erickson, Joe Giovanetto, Jim Gruenewald, Curt Gustafson, Jerry Parker, Todd Ronne, and Chris Walter. I also want to single out Rick Chalupnik, our church's pastor of adult ministries, for the insights he offers week after week as we think through what our church family needs to hear from the sermon text for the following Sunday.

How can I fail to thank my dear friend Dave Goetz for the influence he has had on my life, ministry, and writing. He is truly a "friend who sticks closer than a brother" (Prov. 18:24). Dave is the first editor to give me a shot at writing for publication.

Finally, I am deeply grateful to my wife, Priscilla, who understands the value of the writing ministry God has given me and who encourages me to carve out the time it requires. I love her more than words can say.

Above all, I give thanks for the grace God has given me "through the appearing of our Savior, Christ Jesus, who has destroyed death and has brought life and immortality to light through the gospel" (2 Tim. 1:10). What an incredible privilege to serve as a herald of his gospel. To him be glory and honor forever and ever.

INTRODUCTION

I am not a big fan of editions of the Bible in which the words of Jesus appear in red ink. The red letters imply that the words of Jesus possess greater importance or authority than the words in black letters. But those red letters can serve a symbolic purpose. They suggest how alarming the words of Jesus can be.

There is an interesting relationship between action and speech in the Gospels. Pastors who preach the Gospels will face challenges in each, but this volume will focus on the words in red letters, on the challenges of preaching what Jesus said. This is a book for those who love to preach the gospel from the four Gospels. It is a sequel to my volume *Preaching the Four Gospels with Confidence*. This volume zeros in on preaching the hard sayings of Jesus confidently and persuasively.

Some of these sayings are hard because they are shocking or harsh. Jesus' call for listeners to cut off their hand to avoid the lust that will send them to hell sounds more extreme than a street preacher's "turn or burn." Other sayings are simply confusing. How can Jesus tell a young man who wants to follow him to sell everything he has first and give it to the poor? This does not seem to square with salvation by grace through faith.

Sometimes what Jesus said seems racist or offensive to women, such as the time he responded to a Canaanite woman's request for help by saying, "It is not right to take the children's bread and toss it to the dogs" (Matt. 15:26). But if Jesus' words hold the key to life (John 5:24), then our responsibility as preachers is to understand them truly and proclaim them clearly. This volume aims to help preachers do just that. It will probe nine different categories of Jesus' hard sayings.

There are two ways to read this book. The first is to work your way through it as organized. The other way is to pick and choose the chapters that deal with the most pressing questions you have as you preach the words Jesus taught.

Chapter 1 looks at preaching the harsh and shocking sayings of Jesus. As noted already, in one conversation Jesus appears to call a woman a "dog" (Matt. 15:21–28). In another, Jesus uses the language of cannibalism, imploring his listeners to eat his flesh and drink his blood (John 6:53–58). In yet another discussion, he seems to suggest that he uses parables to obscure the truth rather than to reveal it (Mark 4:11–12). What are we to make of statements that are more revolting and discouraging than they are edifying and encouraging? How can we help our listeners understand them?

Chapter 2 focuses on another perennial problem: "Preaching What Jesus Says about the Radical Demands of Discipleship." It troubles would-be followers of Jesus to hear him say that they must hate their parents (Matt. 10:34–39), skip their father's funeral (Luke 9:61–62), sell everything they own (Luke 18:18–30), and make a daily trek to execution (Luke 9:23). Really? Why would anyone want to follow Jesus under these conditions? And why are they even necessary? Do they apply to Jesus' followers at every place in every time?

2

Chapter 3 considers "Preaching What Jesus Says about Sex and Marriage." What Jesus has to say about lust and marriage seems so out of touch with where Western culture is at the dawn of the twenty-first century. Lust is a national pastime. Marriage is simply an option for men and women who have decided to live together. But there is more difficulty. Jesus' black-and-white comments about divorce have the potential to cause considerable pain to those who have gone through a divorce. Is this what Jesus intended? How can we preach what Jesus said about sex and marriage in a redemptive way?

Chapter 4 explores another challenge: "Preaching What Jesus Says about Hell and Judgment." Everyone agrees that Jesus used some vivid, even terrifying, language. The question is to what extent Jesus' teaching on hell and judgment is metaphorical as opposed to literal. Does Dante's *Inferno* or Jonathan Edwards's fiery pit or Rob Bell's notion of hell reflect what Jesus really taught? Can we offer any hope when preaching Jesus' fiery words?

Chapter 5 examines "Preaching What Jesus Says about the End Times." There are two problems here. One is the fright factor. How can we help listeners process the promises of "great distress, unequaled from the beginning of the world until now" or the warning that the time immediately prior to Jesus' return will be dreadful for pregnant women and nursing mothers (Matt. 24:19–21)? Another problem is that Jesus really did not answer the questions his disciples raised about the end. They wanted to know when it would happen and what would signal his coming. Jesus takes the conversation in a different direction. He skirts their questions and answers the ones he wants to answer. Why?

Chapter 6 enters a theological minefield as it wrestles with "Preaching What Jesus Says about God's Sovereignty and Human Freedom." Sometimes Jesus sounds like a Calvinist. After all, he said: "No one can come to me unless the Father who sent me draws them" (John 6:44). But sometimes Jesus sounds like an Arminian. He also said: "Many will turn away from the faith. . . . but the one who stands firm to the end will be saved" (Matt. 24:10, 13). Whether you are more Arminian or more Calvinistic, how can you preach these texts faithfully so that you lead your listeners to worship rather than confusion and frustration?

Chapter 7 takes on the sticky challenge of "Preaching What Jesus Says about the Law of Moses." Does Jesus set it aside or affirm its ongoing validity? Do the four gospel writers give a consistent perspective when they quote what Jesus said about the Law? Our listeners need to know the answers if they are to figure out what role, if any, the law of Moses plays in their relationship to God.

Chapter 8 turns our attention to "Preaching What Jesus Says about Prayer, Faith, and Miracles." Frankly, what Jesus says about asking and receiving, seeking and finding, knocking and doors opening seems too good to be true. Often when I ask God for my daily bread, it seems that he gives me a rock instead. The idea that my faith can move mountains also seems unrealistic. And the abundance of miracles performed by Jesus makes me wonder where miracles fit into the lives of contemporary Christ-followers. What should we expect from Jesus today?

Finally, chapter 9 addresses "Preaching What Jesus Says to the Pharisees." When you think about it, it seems odd that Jesus reserves his harshest words for a group with whom he had the most in common in theology and piety. In our culture, which values civility and tolerance, what should we make of Jesus' use of epithets like "blind fools," "snakes," and "children of hell" for religious opponents? How can we help our hearers understand the way Jesus treated the Pharisees?

4

Before we begin the journey through these various types of hard sayings, let me emphasize that the aim of this volume is to help preachers be clear, not clever. What did Jesus say, and what did he mean by what he said? Our role is not to tame or whitewash or reinterpret the hard sayings of Jesus. Our aim as preachers is to understand them truly and to proclaim them clearly. Hard sayings get misunderstood easily. But when understood clearly, they have power to put people in motion. The hard sayings of Jesus will pull some of your people closer to Jesus.

They will also drive others away. A few years ago Dan Kimball wrote a book titled *They Like Jesus but Not the Church*. My sense is that when people hear sermons on what Jesus really said, they might walk away saying, "I like Jesus but not his words." They would not be the first. After Jesus' "cannibalism metaphor," "many of his disciples turned back and no longer followed him" (John 6:66). Others affirmed, "You have the words of eternal life. We have come to believe and to know that you are the Holy One of God" (John 6:68–69).

You and I are not responsible for the effect that Jesus' hard words have on our listeners. What we are responsible for is understanding them truly and proclaiming them clearly and faithfully. So let us turn our attention to the faithful proclamation of the hard sayings of Jesus.

1

PREACHING WHAT JESUS SAYS THAT IS HARSH AND SHOCKING

Imagine that you are a speech writer or editor for Jesus during his earthly ministry. Imagine your response when you discover that Jesus plans to say:

> If your right eye causes you to stumble, gouge it out and throw it away. It is better for you to lose one part of your body than for your whole body to be thrown into hell. And if your right hand causes you to stumble, cut it off and throw it away. It is better for you to lose one part of your body than for your whole body to go into hell. (Matt. 5:29–30)

My response might be "Uh, Jesus, this sounds extreme. Do you really think that cutting off body parts is going to help people avoid lust? Do you want to be responsible for people taking you literally and removing eyes and hands and who knows what else?"

Or imagine your horror when you learn what Jesus plans to say to a group of religious leaders: "Very truly I tell you, unless you eat the flesh of the Son of Man and drink his blood, you have no life in you" (John 6:53).

My response would probably be "Jesus, you simply cannot say that! Hyperbole is one thing, but this image crosses the line.

If you talk about eating the flesh of the Son of Man and drinking his blood, you're going to be accused of cannibalism!"

But of course, I am not Jesus' speech writer or editor, and I have no business suggesting that the Son of God tones down his rhetoric or adapts his images to make them more palatable for a contemporary audience.

As a preacher, though, I do have to make Jesus' rhetoric and his images intelligible to a contemporary audience. So how can preachers handle the things we wish Jesus had never said? Throughout this volume, we will explore how to preach various hard sayings of Jesus, but this chapter will zero in on those sayings that are particularly harsh or shocking. How do we handle them in our preaching?

When Jesus Uses Hyperbole

Some of Jesus' harsh, shocking sayings can be accounted for by his use of hyperbole. While I encourage preachers not to use "shop talk" in their sermons, I make an exception here. When preaching on a particularly shocking saying of Jesus, I will use the word *hyperbole*. To lighten the mood, I will tell my listeners that I am a bit afraid of using a word like this because it might require me to charge them tuition! But the word is a useful one. It means simply "deliberate exaggeration." Then I will say something like, "Hearing the words *Jesus* and *exaggeration* together might put you on edge, but this is a legitimate communication technique that Jesus used."

So what exactly is this technique? Leland Ryken offers a helpful explanation. You might use some or all of this when you explain hyperbole to your listeners. Ryken writes:

How should we understand such exaggerations? We must avoid foolish attempts to press them into literal statements. Hyperbole does not express literal, factual truth. Instead it expresses emotional truth. Hyperbole is the voice of conviction. It captures the spirit of an event or inner experience. After all, when do people use hyperbole in ordinary discourse? They use it either when they feel strongly about something ("I wrote till my hand fell off") or when they are trying to be persuasive ("*Everybody* agrees that the test was unfair").[1]

Ryken's explanation of hyperbole reminds us how our listeners need to understand that Jesus is merely doing what *they* do to emphasize a point. For example, you might say, "When my son first learned to drive, I told him a thousand times not to text while driving." The exact figure may have been only seventy-three, but the exaggeration dramatizes the point. So does a statement like "I would sell my car and walk to the United Center to hear Taylor Swift in concert." If I make a statement like that, no one expects to see a "for sale" sign on my car, nor do they expect to see me walking along Interstate 94 to make the thirty-nine-mile trip from my home in the Chicago suburbs to the venue in downtown Chicago. They understand that I am simply passionate and intentional about attending the concert.

Taking Extreme Measures to Deal with Lust

One of Jesus' more extreme uses of hyperbole occurs in Matthew 5:29–30 when he warns his listeners about lust. Even though Origen "applied" this text to his life by castrating himself,[2] most modern commentators recognize that "literal self-mutilation is not Christ's objective."[3] This is hyperbole that emphasizes the need for drastic action. Followers of Jesus must deal radically with their sin.[4] Haddon Robinson provides a good example of how we might explain this to our listeners:

> To interpret Christ's words about mutilation literally can be almost humorous. Suppose I'm having a struggle with lust. I poke out my right eye, but no evidence shows that one-eyed people are less lustful than two-eyed people. I'll chop off my right hand, but no studies verify that one-handed people are less lustful than two-handed people. I could gouge out my left eye, but sexual fantasies will still play on the cinema of my mind. Even if I'm blind, I could go the whole way—amputate both arms and both legs—but torsos are not exempt from lust.
>
> The problem isn't body parts. Jesus used absurdity to show that adultery, like all sin, is serious enough for men and women to end up in hell. We ought to deal drastically with anything that leads us to that.[5]

But listeners need help seeing what drastic action looks like in the twenty-first century. So Robinson continues: "If our magazine reading or our cable TV watching causes us to lust, then we need to cancel our subscriptions."[6] Robinson offered these suggestions in 1988, before the popularity of the Internet exploded. Drastic action today will certainly take it into account as Grant Osborne suggests in his application of this text:

> Jesus' call for extreme measures must be heeded before it is too late. Adults as well as children should purchase the software to lock themselves out of X-rated sites, and accountability groups need to be set up in every church. All too many males (as well as many females) should be admitting, "I am a sexoholic," and should be getting help. This issue has become

a pandemic, and every church and Christian group should be seeking solutions even more vigorously than in the past.[7]

The Language of Cannibalism

John 6 contains another radical and even revolting use of hyperbole. Beginning in John 6:32, Jesus launches into a rabbinic argument in which he claims to be the food that leads to eternal life. This took place after Jesus fed the five thousand (vv. 1–15) and when the crowd following Jesus essentially asked him if he was duplicating what Moses did (vv. 30–32). In Second Temple Judaism, there was an expectation that the Messiah would provide bread in the same way that Moses had provided manna. *Second Baruch*, a text dating to about A.D. 100, describes the condition on the whole earth when the Messiah, the Anointed One, is revealed. Food will be so plentiful that "those who are hungry will enjoy themselves and they will, moreover, see marvels every day" (*2 Bar.* 29:6). Even more striking is this description: "And it will happen at that time that the treasury of manna will come down again from on high, and they will eat of it in those years because these are they who will have arrived at the consummation of time" (*2 Bar.* 29:8).

Jesus, then, declares: "I am the bread of life. Whoever comes to me will never go hungry, and whoever believes in me will never be thirsty. . . . For my Father's will is that everyone who looks to the Son and believes in him shall have eternal life, and I will raise them up at the last day" (John 6:35, 40). This statement elicited grumbling. The grumbling in John 6:41 and later in the account, in verse 61, recalls the grumbling of Exodus 16:2. There, the people grumbled *before* receiving the manna. Here in John 6 the people grumbled *after* they received it. It seems to be this grumbling that prompts Jesus to radicalize his metaphor. According to John 6:51, Jesus said: "I am the living bread that came down from heaven. Whoever eats this bread will live forever. This bread is my flesh, which I will give for the life of the world."

Now Jesus had his listeners really upset! John 6:52 reports: "Then the Jews began to argue sharply among themselves, 'How can this man give us his flesh to eat?'" In response to this question, Jesus pushes their sensibilities to the limit with a response that can only be described as "hyperbole gone wild."

> Jesus said to them, "Very truly I tell you, unless you eat the flesh of the Son of Man and drink his blood, you have no life in you. Whoever eats my flesh and drinks my blood has eternal life, and I will raise them up at the last day. For my flesh is real food and my blood is real drink. Whoever eats my flesh and drinks my blood remains in me, and I in them. Just as the living Father sent me and I live because of the Father, so the one who feeds on me will live because of me. This is the bread that came down from heaven. Your ancestors ate manna and died, but whoever feeds on this bread will live forever." (vv. 53–58)

So how do we explain this to our contemporary listeners? To be sure, we use the eating and drinking metaphor in contemporary culture, talking about how we devour a book or swallow a story or drink in beauty or chew on an idea. But Jesus pushes this kind of imagery to its limits when he calls his listeners to eat his flesh and drink his blood. This simply sounds cannibalistic and grotesque! Yes, and that is exactly the way Jesus intended it to sound. Craig Keener argues that "When Jesus speaks of eating his flesh (6:51–53), he invites disgust from his contemporaries."[8]

There was a method to this madness, though. His radical language intended to convey the radical identity and intimacy with Jesus needed to experience his provision for our deepest longings. What made the imagery appropriate, though borderline, is the connection to Passover—the setting for John 6 (see v. 4). Keener explains: "In the context of Passover (6:4), however, the image most naturally evoked is that of the paschal lamb. Thus, for example, rabbinic texts concerning the Passover speak of eating flesh (the lamb) and drinking the blood of grapes (cups at Passover), here perhaps applicable to Jesus as the true vine (15:1)."[9] This is a stunning way, then, to speak of embracing or believing in Jesus' death. The symbolism must be understood in terms of Jesus' repeated calls for belief in him (see John 6:35, 40, 47, 69). Such stunning teaching demands a response. Some followers grumble, turn back, and no longer follow Jesus (vv. 60–66). But Jesus' true disciples recognize that he is the Holy One of God who has the words of eternal life (vv. 66–71).

In both Matthew 5:29–30 and John 6:54–57 we have seen that Jesus uses hyperbolic language to make sure he makes his point. This is not shocking language for the sake of simply shocking or unnerving people. Rather, Jesus' use of hyperbole reflects the passion and conviction behind the message he proclaimed. The message was important enough to use whatever heightened language he could to get across his point.

But how can we tell whether a particular statement is hyperbolic or not? For example, at the end of one of his parables, Jesus says that worthless servants who do not steward their talents will be thrown "outside, into the darkness, where there will be weeping and gnashing of teeth" (Matt. 25:30). How can we tell if this is simply harsh reality or if it is hyperbole?

Leland Ryken provides a helpful way of distinguishing between hyperbole and a harsh statement that should be taken at face value. He observes that hyperbole "advertises its lack of literal truth."[10] It is obviously a figure of speech since it would make no sense taken literally. This is certainly the case with Jesus' statement about eating his flesh and drinking his blood. These images went against the theology and sensibility of the Jewish people to whom Jesus spoke.

But Jesus' words about judgment, as harsh as they are, fit with the theology of the Scriptures he and his listeners held dear. To be sure, the image of "outer darkness" and "weeping and gnashing of teeth" is heightened language and, thus, poetic. But these are stock ways of describing both the removal of sinners from God's presence and the anguish that accompanies it.[11] There is nothing about these statements that advertises a lack of literal truth the way that Jesus' call for cutting off limbs does when he speaks about curbing lust.

Here is another instance where commentaries can help. The point is not to let commentators do all of our thinking for us. But I want to know what Bible scholars throughout the history of the church have concluded about particular sayings of Jesus that strike me as hyperbole. Both asking whether a statement advertises its lack of literal truth and listening to a long tradition of godly interpreters will help me assess whether a given statement of Jesus' is simply "harsh but real" or, in fact, hyperbolic.

Did Jesus Use Racist Language?

Now we turn to a different type of harsh, shocking speech. In Matthew 15:21–28, we read the account of a Canaanite woman coming to Jesus and crying out for mercy for her demonized daughter who was suffering terribly (v. 22). But "Jesus did not answer a word" (v. 23). When he finally speaks, he says, "I was sent only to the lost sheep of Israel" (v. 24). But the woman was persistent. She came and knelt before him and said, "Lord, help me!" (v. 25). It is at this point that Jesus says something that seems utterly offensive. He replies: "It is not right to take the children's bread and toss it to the dogs" (v. 26). This statement is shocking not because it is hyperbolic but because it seems rude, insensitive, chauvinistic, and even racist given the fact that the woman was a Canaanite and that Jesus had indicated how he had been sent to the lost sheep of Israel.

Some try to soften Jesus' words by observing that the diminutive form of the word indicates that Jesus has in view a "little dog" and that the word thus implies the affection one might have for a pet dog as opposed to a wild dog. But that misses the point; dogs were unclean animals. R. T. France correctly responds: "It is true that the Greek term is a diminutive, but only a pet-loving Western culture would suggest that this reduces the offense; a "little dog" is no less unclean than a big one! The woman's reply takes these to be house dogs rather than street dogs, but that does little to alleviate the problem."[12] The fact is, Jesus has used a pejorative image in reference to someone of another race. "References to dogs in biblical literature are overwhelmingly negative, and when the term is used metaphorically for human beings, it is abusive and derogatory."[13]

So Jesus seems to share the same derogatory attitude that the majority in his race (Jewish) held toward Gentiles. But that conclusion will not stand up for at least two reasons. First, Jesus' prophetic words in Matthew 8:11–12 have established his vision of a multiethnic people of God. Second, the exorcism in the region of the Gadarenes (Matt 8:28–34) demonstrates that Jesus is not reluctant to deal with demon possession in a Gentile context.[14]

Context, then, is everything when it comes to meaning. France's argument is confirmed by one more glance at the context. The woman replies to Jesus' shocking statement with this observation: "Even the dogs eat the crumbs that fall from their master's table" (15:27). Jesus then replies: "Woman, you have great faith! Your request is granted." Matthew 15:28 reports that the woman's "daughter was healed at that moment." Here, France suggests that Jesus intended this outcome from the start: A good teacher may sometimes aim to draw out a pupil's best insight by a deliberate challenge that does not necessarily represent the teacher's own view—even if the phrase "devil's advocate" may not be quite appropriate to this context.[15]

So Jesus provoked the woman in a good way to elicit and even highlight her remarkable faith. This is a poignant reminder that we cannot jump to quick conclusions about sayings of Jesus that seem offensive and shocking. Rather than finding superficial ways of wiggling out of the difficulty, we must be patient and locate these sayings in the wider context of what Jesus was all about as the herald of good news.

A Case of Hard-Line Theology

We have looked so far at two kinds of statements that are quite revolting. The first kind uses a type of hyperbole that is either absurd or grotesque. The second kind of statement uses imagery that seems to reek of racism. The next statement to which we turn is shocking for its harshness. It seems rather "remarkable because one of the glories of the biblical faith is the great emphasis Scripture lays on the graciousness and wideness of God's forgiveness (for example, Pss 65:3; 86:5; 130:3–4; Isa 1:18; Mic 7:19; 1 Jn 1:7)."[16] In this saying, Jesus speaks of blasphemy against the Spirit and describes it as "the unpardonable sin." All three Synoptic Gospels record this saying (see Matt. 12:31–32; Mark 3:28–30; Luke 12:10). Matthew 12:31–32 records Jesus as saying:

> And so I tell you, every kind of sin and slander can be forgiven, but blasphemy against the Spirit will not be forgiven. Anyone who speaks a word against the Son of Man will be forgiven, but anyone who speaks against the Holy Spirit will not be forgiven, either in this age or in the age to come.

What should we say to listeners who fear that they may have blasphemed the Spirit when Jesus clearly says that this is the one sin that will not be forgiven? The obvious place to begin is with a definition of the word itself. Blasphemy is extreme slander.[17] It refers to "some form of profaning God's name."[18] I sometimes describe blasphemy for my listeners as dragging God's name and reputation through the mud.

Next, I find it helpful to point listeners to the context. Osborne comments on Matthew 12:31, noting that "the introductory 'because of this' (διὰ τοῦτο [dia touto]) links this not just with v. 30 but with all of vv. 24–30, that is, the conflict between Jesus and the Pharisees."[19] The Pharisees have been questioning the source of power that enabled Jesus to drive out demons from people. In sum, they have been attributing the work of the Spirit to Satan in a way that reflects rebellion against what is indisputable rather than ignorance or mere unbelief.[20]

This leads to a third observation. The sin in question is more than a lapse by a follower of Jesus who momentarily denies Jesus as Peter did.[21] It is even more than the persistent unbelief and hostility toward Jesus as Saul displayed before his dramatic conversion.[22] Both the reinstatement of Peter and the conversion of Saul make this clear.

Taking these three observations into account, what, then, is the unforgivable sin? Blomberg answers: "Probably blasphemy against the Holy Spirit is nothing more or less than the unrelenting rejection of his advances."[23]

Bock adds a further nuance that helps clarify the distinction between speaking against the Son of Man and speaking against the Holy Spirit. Commenting on Luke 12:10, he argues that "blasphemy of the Spirit is not so much an act of rejection as it is a persistent and decisive rejection of the Spirit's message and work concerning Jesus. When a person obstinately rejects and fixedly refuses that message or evidence, that person is not forgiven."[24]Bock further notes that this understanding of Jesus' saying about blasphemy against the Spirit "looks at the totality of a person's response to the Spirit, not just a moment in it. If single moments were in view, then Peter and Paul would fall into this category."[25]Understood in this way, the nature of the sin is defined not so much by the one against whom it is committed— either against Jesus or against the Spirit—but by the level or depth of the rejection. According to Blomberg, "probably blasphemy against the Holy Spirit is nothing more or less than the unrelenting rejection of his advances. Jesus' teaching thus parallels Acts 4:12. If one rejects the Spirit of God in Jesus, there is no one else in all the cosmos who can provide salvation."[26]Along with this explanation, a wise preacher will help listeners apply this saying properly. As the old adage says, good preaching comforts the afflicted and afflicts the comfortable. Without giving a false sense of assurance, we must comfort those who live in fear that they have committed the unpardonable sin. The first time I ever preached through the Gospel of Mark, I ran across some solid pastoral advice in C. E. B. Cranfield's commentary. I marked it in my copy of his commentary more than twenty-five years ago, and I still follow it today. Cranfield wrote: "It is a matter of great importance pastorally that we can say with absolute confidence to anyone who is overwhelmed by the fear that he has committed this sin, that the fact that he is so troubled is itself a sure proof that he has not committed it."[27] Yes, worry over whether one has committed this sin or not makes it quite clear that they have not; the defiance and obstinacy attached to this sin leaves no room for those committing it to doubt themselves!

On the other hand, our preaching needs to afflict those who are all too comfortable about attributing this sin to others. Blomberg comments: "We dare never label anyone as having committed this sin. Only God knows human hearts, and we would often make the wrong guess."[28] How can we tell if a particular opponent of the gospel will turn out like Saul of Tarsus or turn out to be someone who has truly blasphemed the Spirit? Only God knows.

Hiding the Truth from People Who Need It Most

There is one more shocking saying of Jesus that is worth our attention since it lurks in the background every time we preach a parable of Jesus. Perhaps we have grown so used to this saying that it has lost a bit of its shock value. But how in the world can Jesus respond to a question about his parables with this explanation?

The secret of the kingdom of God has been given to you. But to those on the outside everything is said in parables so that,

> "they may be ever seeing but never perceiving,
>   and ever hearing but never understanding;
> otherwise they might turn and be forgiven!"
>   (Mark 4:11–12)

Klyne Snodgrass identifies the problem we have with this text, along with the parallel passages in Matthew 13:13–17 and Luke 8:10:

> It would be easier to ignore these verses. The language is difficult and harsh and appears to say that Jesus tells parables to keep people from understanding so that they will not repent and be forgiven—the exact opposite of everything we know both about Jesus and parables. Not surprisingly, these verses are omitted in the standard lectionary for preaching.[29]So how can we help our listeners make sense of what sounds a bit like nonsense? The key to understanding what Jesus says about his parables concealing truth is his quotation of Isaiah 6:9–10. All three Synoptic Gospels record Jesus' quotation of it. Snodgrass begins by noting how these words functioned in their original context: "The intent is not that Isaiah actually should do what these verses say, and he does not. The lack of hearing and seeing has already been accomplished. Still, even though the nation is too far gone, Isaiah urges people to stop being rebellious and turn to God."[30]Jesus uses Isaiah 6:9–10 in line with its intent: to urge hearing in a context where judgment is assured. The words of Isaiah 6:9–10 "express by hyperbole what has already happened due to hardness of heart and unwillingness to hear."[31]Carson makes another helpful point that preachers will want to explain to

their listeners. Commenting on Matthew's account of this saying, he writes:

If Jesus simply wished to hide the truth from the outsiders, he need never have spoken to them. His concern for mission (9:35–38; 10:1–10; 28:16–20) excludes that idea. So he must preach without casting his pearls before pigs (7:6). He does so in parables: that is, in such a way as to harden and reject those who are hard of heart and to enlighten—often with further explanation—his disciples.... Thus the parables spoken to the crowds do not simply convey information or mask it, but challenge the hearers.[32] Finally, David Wenham offers a helpful summary that preachers can use or adapt when helping their listeners grasp the role of parables as revealers and concealers of truth. His summary consists of six statements:

1. Parables are designed and intended to teach people about the kingdom of God, that is, to be an effective medium of communication.
2. But parables are not so simple and unambiguous that no one could mistake their meaning: in fact, only some "get" the meaning of parables (their interpretation); others do not.
3. This is the pattern of Jesus' ministry as a whole: some see and respond to the mystery of the kingdom revealed in Jesus; some are blind and refuse to do so.
4. The disciples' understanding of the mystery is not their own achievement, but the gift of God.
5. The outsiders' failure to understand is a sign of God's judgment on people's hardness of heart, as it was in the prophetic ministry of people such as Isaiah.

6. Jesus parabolic ministry therefore comes as God's gift to some and his judgment to others. We might paraphrase the difficult saying: "To you, the disciples, God has given understanding of the mysteries of the kingdom of God—the kingdom brought and taught by Jesus—and so you receive interpretation of the parables to expand your understanding; to those on the outside there are parables only, so that they fail to see or hear the mystery of the kingdom, receiving instead the divine judgment spoken of by Isaiah."[33]

A Surprising Friendship

When Bill Clinton was elected to the presidency, no one expected him to form a friendship with former President Richard Nixon. Certainly not Nixon, who spent the months after Clinton's election trying everything short of voodoo to get Clinton's attention.[34] But a surprising friendship developed. After Nixon died, Clinton lamented that it felt like the loss of his mother. In an interview, he said: "Just today I had a problem, and I said to the person working with me, 'I wish I could pick up the phone and call Richard Nixon and ask him what he thinks we ought to do about this.'"[35] In a similar way, preachers who are leery of preaching the shocking, harsh sayings of Jesus may eventually develop a friendship with them. The reason for this is that these sayings infuse a sermon with tension. I have often heard Haddon Robinson say, "Tension is your friend, not your enemy. When the tension is over, so is your sermon." The tension created by the harsh, shocking sayings of Jesus will not only keep people listening but will agitate them to the point of really hearing the challenge Jesus is making.

Jesus knew what he was doing when he used harsh, shocking language. We need to understand what he was doing and help our listeners understand it, too, so that we hear "loud and clear" the challenges he issues to us.

2

PREACHING WHAT JESUS SAYS ABOUT THE RADICAL DEMANDS OF DISCIPLESHIP

Dietrich Bonhoeffer has captured the radical demands of discipleship in a chilling, memorable sentence. In his classic *The Cost of Discipleship*, Bonhoeffer wrote: "When Christ calls a man, he bids him come and die."[1] Indeed, Bonhoeffer's allegiance to Christ set him on a journey that ended in execution at a prison camp in Flossenbürg, Germany, on April 9, 1945. Years later, the camp doctor, H. Fischer-Hüllstrung, gave the following account of Bonhoeffer's last minutes alive:

> Through the half-open door in one room of the huts I saw Pastor Bonhoeffer, before taking off his prison garb, kneeling on the floor praying fervently to his God. I was most deeply moved by the way this lovable man prayed, so devout and so certain that God heard his prayer. At the place of execution, he again said a short prayer and then climbed the steps to the gallows, brave and composed. His death ensued after a few seconds. In the almost fifty years that I worked as a doctor, I have hardly ever seen a man die so entirely submissive to the will of God.[2]

Some have questioned Bonhoeffer's status as a martyr since he was executed for his role in a plot to assassinate Hitler rather than for professed allegiance to Christ. However, Bonhoeffer clearly saw his attempts to topple Hitler as an outworking of his commitment to follow Jesus Christ. Though he hoped to live, to marry his fiancée, Maria Von Wedemeyer, and to continue the fight against cheap grace ("the deadly enemy of our Church"[3]), Bonhoeffer submitted to death, acting out the conviction he had so eloquently expressed: "When Christ calls a man, he bids him come and die."

But at the dawn of the twenty-first century, followers of Jesus may find such a claim grandiose—at least for those living in North America. Quite frankly, following Jesus does not put many Westerners at risk of death. Believers on their way to places of worship on Sundays may worry about losing their lives in auto accidents, but they do not worry about losing their lives for assembling to worship Christ. Some may have legitimate concerns about losing jobs for their commitment to Christ, but not their physical lives. All of this leads to uneasiness when we set out to preach what Jesus says about the radical demands of discipleship.

However, the uneasiness runs much deeper. How can Jesus call his followers to hate their parents, to die daily, to refuse to say good-bye to family, and sell all their possessions? What does this even look like in contemporary culture? Preachers must have a handle on these questions whenever they preach the texts in which Jesus offers such radical demands. In this chapter, we will explore four rather outrageous requirements Jesus makes for following him and reflect on how we might preach them.

Hating Your Relatives

One of Jesus' requirements hits us where it hurts the most—the area of family. Like you, there is nothing more precious to me on this earth than my family. My wife and I recently dropped off our youngest son at college, and all three of us cried when we said good-bye. As much as we look forward to this new chapter of our son's life, there is pain in the separation because we love being together. For us, the highlights of last year and next year center around family gatherings. So it is quite disconcerting for me to read what Jesus says in Matthew 10:34–39:

> Do not suppose that I have come to bring peace to the earth. I did not come to bring peace, but a sword. For I have come to turn
>
>> "a man against his father,
>>> a daughter against her mother,
>> a daughter-in-law against her mother-in-law—
>>> a man's enemies will be the members of his own household."
>
> Anyone who loves their father or mother more than me is not worthy of me; anyone who loves their son or daughter more than me is not worthy of me. Whoever does not take up their cross and follow me is not worthy of me. Whoever finds their life will lose it, and whoever loses their life for my sake will find it.

If this seems extreme, it only gets worse in Luke 14:26 where Jesus says: "If anyone comes to me and does not hate father and mother, wife and children, brothers and sisters—yes, even their own life—such a person cannot be my disciple."

How are we to understand these words? We can come to grips with them and help our listeners do so as well when we note the following facts. First, although peace is the result of the salvation Jesus is bringing, "the mission to the lost world will not result in peace for those who take the gospel to the world."⁴ This is the point of Matthew 10:34–36 in which Jesus quotes from Micah 7:6—a description of the sinfulness and rebellion in the time of King Ahaz that points to an even worse situation in Jesus' time. The world is so sinful and rebellious that family members dishonor each other. Jesus' ultimate purpose is, of course, to bring peace to the world (see Matt. 5:9; 10:12–13; Luke 2:14; John 14:27; 20:19, 21, 26). But in the short-term, his coming has the opposite effect on people.

Second, Jesus is not calling his followers *not* to love their parents or children. Rather, he is calling his followers not to love parents or children "more than (Greek *hyper*: above) me." Other passages in the Gospels show that Jesus recognizes and encourages familial love (see Matt. 15:4–6; 19:19). So the question concerns where a Christ-follower's ultimate allegiance lies. Family is a wonderful gift from God, but the temptation is to turn it into an idol that replaces God and the love that he alone can provide.

Third, the requirement to "hate" family members, expressed in Luke 14:26, must be understood as "not literal but rhetorical."⁵ It is a Semitic expression that has to do more with choice than emotion. Darrell L. Bock explains: "Otherwise, Jesus' command to love one's neighbor as oneself as a summation of what God desires makes no sense (Luke 10:25–37). The call to hate simply means to 'love less' (Gen. 29:30–31; Deut. 21:15–17; Judg. 14:16). The image is strong, but it is not a call to be insensitive or to leave all feelings behind."⁶ Once again, a consideration of the historical-cultural context brings the meaning into sharper focus. Bock writes:

> This saying [Luke 14:26] needs to be set in the context of its first-century setting. At that time a Jewish person who

made a choice for Jesus would alienate his or her family. If someone desired acceptance by family more than a relationship with God, one might never come to Jesus, given the rejection that would inevitably follow. In other words, there could be no casual devotion to Jesus in the first century.... Contemporary comparisons may be seen in certain formerly Communist Eastern European settings, in Moslem countries, or in tight-knit Asian families.[7]

In fact, I know Asian and Indian Christ-followers in the congregations I pastored who have faced this harsh reality. Their families have disowned them for the decision to follow Christ.

We will help our listeners when we clarify that a decision to follow Christ will result in greater, truer love for our families. Yes, there will be more love for our families, not less. But this is a love that flows from our commitment to Christ. What Jesus warns about is a love for our families that eclipses our love for him. The issue is where our ultimate allegiance lies.

Skipping Your Father's Funeral

Another requirement of discipleship cuts even deeper into the hearts of those Christ-followers who have had loved ones die. I am writing this paragraph exactly ten years after my father breathed his last breath on earth. Maynard Mathewson, my dad, died on August 13, 2002, just a few weeks shy of his sixty-third birthday. He had been battling cancer for almost two years. We thought he was making progress, but a week before his death I received word that his health was rapidly deteriorating. I was attending a church camp in the mountains of Montana when I got this news. Thanks to a friend who had some extra frequent flyer miles, I managed to return to central Illinois and spend his last two days with him. I was sitting beside his bed when he died. Then my three brothers and I planned and officiated his funeral. When I think about my dad's funeral, I remember how painful it was to attend and officiate it. But I simply cannot imagine missing it. The pain of missing it would have been more than I could bear.

Yet this is precisely what Jesus offers to one man as a requirement for discipleship. Matthew 8:21–22 records the conversation:

> Another disciple said to him, "Lord, first let me go and bury my father."
>
> But Jesus told him, "Follow me, and let the dead bury their own dead."

This follows a conversation in which a scribe promises to follow Jesus wherever Jesus goes, and then Jesus warns the man that he (Jesus) lacks the comforts of home. In the first instance, Jesus deals with the problem of "overeagerness"; in the second instance, in which Jesus challenges a would-be follower to "let the dead bury their own dead," the problem is "undereagerness."[8] Or, to put it another way, the first man who comes to Jesus "promises too much (what he cannot deliver) while the second promises too little (what he does not want to sacrifice)."[9]

What, then, do we make of Jesus' challenge to let someone else bury his father? In first century, sons were expected to honor their parents by attending to their parents' burial.[10] One approach is to understand the man's request and Jesus' reply as referring to the period of waiting until one's living father, presumably aged, has died and can be buried. In such a case, the expression may be an idiom for "let me wait until my father is dead."[11] Another possibility is that the man is returning to fulfill a second stage of burial duties, where he takes his father's bones from a slab in the family tomb and places them in an ossuary—a small box used as a receptacle for the bones of a deceased person.[12] However, David Turner may well be right when he says that "such conjecture may only distract the reader from the rigor of Jesus's words."[13] Jesus is probably speaking to a man whose father has just died and is about to be buried. Whatever the case, Jesus' words are at odds with the cultural expectations for sons to take care of the burial of their fathers.

What we likely have here is a case of hyperbole. This does not diminish the force of Jesus' words but recognizes that Jesus' concern is much larger than whether or not disciples attend their fathers' funerals. This seems to be confirmed by the Gospel of Luke, which records the same conversation in 9:59–60 and then includes a different yet similar piece of dialogue:

> Still another said, "I will follow you, Lord; but first let me go back and say goodbye to my family."

> Jesus replied, "No one who puts a hand to the plow and looks back is fit for service in the kingdom of God." (vv. 61–62)

Whatever gets in the way of total commitment to Jesus Christ must be abandoned. If that is making burial arrangements for a parent, then so be it. If funeral arrangements do not stand in the way, then we need not insist categorically that all disciples must stay away from their parents' funerals to show allegiance to Jesus Christ. Something like attending a funeral becomes an obstacle to overcome when it becomes an excuse for delaying or diminishing our efforts to follow Christ.

This is precisely the situation in a third requirement for discipleship that seems outrageous and excessive.

Selling Everything You Own

All three Synoptic Gospels record a conversation in which Jesus' answer to the question of how a person receives eternal life seems downright confusing. Located in Matthew 19:16–30, Mark 10:17–31, and Luke 18:18–30, the conversation takes place between Jesus and "the rich, young ruler." Matthew tells us the man was young. All three Synoptics inform us that he was wealthy. Luke describes him as a ruler. The discussion began when this man asked Jesus what he must do to inherit eternal life.

Whenever I preach this account, I tell my listeners that I know how Jesus *should* answer the question. Jesus has a wonderful illustration at his disposal. In all three Gospels, the prior pericope recounts Jesus' blessing of the children. Mark and Luke include Jesus' challenge for his listeners to receive the kingdom of God like a child or else they will not enter it (Mark 10:15; Luke 18:17). Matthew omits this, presumably because he already included it in 18:3–4. So I would expect Jesus to say something like: "It's interesting that you would ask this question, because I was just talking about it. What I emphasized was that you can inherit eternal life by exercising childlike faith."

But Jesus does not do this. Instead he brings up the Ten Commandments and gives the impression that if this guy has kept them, then he has eternal life. This answer seems to muddy the water. It seems like Jesus is contradicting what he said earlier about childlike faith.

But Jesus knows exactly what he is doing. Jesus is, in fact, saying, "If you have obeyed all the commands, you will receive eternal life." Yet he knows full well that neither this young man nor anyone else has kept all of God's commands. The young man, however, does not understand this. He resembles the folks in Luke 18:9 who *were confident of their own righteousness.* So Jesus' talk about the Ten Commandments is not sloppy, confused theology. Rather, Jesus is trying to expose this man's confidence in his own righteousness.

When that does not work, Jesus turns to another tactic, and we must understand it as a tactic or we will misread what he says next. According to Luke 18:22, Jesus said: "You still lack one thing. Sell everything you have and give to the poor, and you will have treasure in heaven. Then come, follow me." In a recent sermon on Luke 18:18–30, I handled verse 22 like this:

> All right, what do we make of this, in light of what Jesus has already said about faith? In Luke 17:19, Jesus said to the leper, "Your faith has made you well." In Luke 18:8, he says: "When the Son of Man comes, will he find faith on the earth?" Now it sounds like he's telling us we have to buy our salvation, doesn't it? But that's not what Jesus is doing. He is exposing what is keeping this ruler from exercising genuine faith and following him. Jesus knows that if this man, or anyone else, is attached to wealth, then they will be pulled away from Jesus. If wealth is where your allegiance is, then your faith is really not faith.

> Still, I have to confess that part of me says, "Jesus, are you kidding? That sounds so radical!" But I take very seriously what Jesus has said, and I want to get it right, even if it's painful for me and for you. If I neuter or water down what Jesus has said, that would be dishonest with the text of Scripture, and I would be distorting what my Lord has said.

David Platt has written a fine, but discomforting, book titled *Radical*. Platt is a pastor in Alabama, and his book is a *New York Times* bestseller. You can tell from the title that Platt wants to come to grips with the radical life to which Jesus calls us. And in his book, he wrestles with this account—the version found in the Gospel of Mark, but the same account, same conversation.[14] Platt says there are a couple of errors we must avoid when we read this hard saying of Jesus. One is to assume that Jesus *always* asks people to sell everything. It's not quite that simple. That doesn't seem to be the picture we get in the New Testament. There were wealthy believers who used their funds to support the apostle Paul's ministry. They had obviously not sold everything to follow Christ. I notice in Luke 19:8–9 that when Zacchaeus gave half—50 percent, not 100 percent!—of his possessions to the poor, Jesus commended him and said, "Today salvation has come to this house." But before you breathe a sigh of relief, Platt identifies a second error, and that is to assume that Jesus *never* asks people to sell everything. He certainly does here. What Jesus calls all of us to do is to detach ourselves from our wealth. The way that works out may be different. But if we're not willing to let go of our wealth, it's going to drag us down to hell!

At this point, having explained what the text meant, I turned to how it applies to modern listeners like us. To make the point, I began by briefly retelling my listeners a legend about a group of ancient warriors who held their battle-axes out of the water when they were baptized. They didn't do this because they were afraid their battle-axes would get wet and rust. No, they were declaring: "Christ, you can have my life. I commit myself fully to you. Except for one thing. I'm going to go on killing people in battle. I'm not going to give that up for you." I told my listeners that this legend reminds me of what we are tempted to do when we are baptized, when we make a commitment to follow Christ. Many of us, I fear, hold something out of the water in our hands when we are baptized. Not literally, but in our hearts.

What we hold out of the water may vary, but it invariably comes back to wealth. It might be our debit cards, representing the control over our bank accounts. It might be the title to a lake house in Georgia or a condo near a Colorado ski resort. It might be tickets to a Broadway play or season tickets to NFL games. It might be the photos of the living room furniture we want to purchase. Whatever the case, Jesus is arguing that you cannot receive the gift of eternal life if you cannot give up your wealth.

Those are hard words. They have nothing to do with buying or earning eternal life. They have everything to do with genuine faith, a faith that trusts Jesus and is willing to submit to him in every area of life. When we explain and apply them well, our listeners will understand that Jesus is not speaking nonsense. But neither is he diminishing the radical demands of following him.

A Daily Trek to Execution

A final requirement for discipleship that seems extreme is the one Dietrich Bonhoeffer seized upon when he challenged would-be followers of Jesus in his own day with the line: "When Christ calls a man, he bids him come and die." Jesus expressed this requirement in Luke 9:23: "Then he said to them all: 'Whoever wants to be my disciple must deny themselves and take up their cross daily and follow me.'"

The key to understanding this rather revolting, shocking image is to notice what it images. The act of cross bearing—a visible, public affair that pictured a criminal's humility before the state—serves as an image of self-denial. That is Jesus' concern. Bock explains: "The essence of saving trust in God is self-denial, a recognition that he must save because disciples cannot save themselves, that life must be given over into God's care and protection. Disciples do not respond to their own personal wills, but to God's."[15]

Wise pastors need to drill this idea into their own hearts and minds, as well as the hearts and minds of their listeners. The reason for this, as Eugene Peterson observes, is that "the 'text' that seems to be most in favor on the American landscape today is the sovereign self."[16] When a self-serving, self-centered approach to life bleeds over into Christianity, following Christ gets reduced to a quest to make my life better. Jesus becomes the teacher or guru or spiritual leader who helps me actualize my life. To be sure, Jesus did say, "I have come that they may have life, and have it to the full" (John 10:10). But following Jesus is not only an invitation to "get a life," it is an invitation to lose it. Christ, rather than self, must be the disciple's pursuit and longing and joy and satisfaction.

A couple of other details deserve attention, and we will do well to point them out to our listeners when we preach on Luke 9:23. First, the cross taken up by disciples is *their* cross.[17] This is not at all to disassociate it with the cross of Jesus Christ. Rather, the idea is that followers of Jesus Christ, like their master, have their particular burdens to bear as a direct result of following Christ. Perhaps our listeners need to hear us say that the image of "cross bearing" is referring to more than a demanding boss, chronic arthritis, a wayward child, or an investment gone sour.

These are real, disconcerting circumstances. But they happen to nonbelievers or less committed believers as well as to those who rigorously pursue Jesus. The cross we bear for following Christ will be something like a boss who demeans us for our Christian witness or a family member who rejects us because of our love for Jesus. Second, I am struck by how this cross bearing is something we do every single day as followers of Jesus. True followers are willing not simply to face lone, isolated, one-time blows for following Jesus; they trek to the place of execution, figuratively speaking, on a daily basis.

No Cheap Grace

What is hard for listeners—and those who preach to them!—to grasp is that Christ's salvation is absolutely free, but it may cost us all we claim is ours. Of course, we cannot earn God's grace, for it is free. Yet we dare not cheapen it by obscuring the level of commitment and self-abandonment required for those who would follow Jesus and experience his grace. As Dietrich Bonhoeffer wrote in *The Cost of Discipleship*, "Cheap grace is the deadly enemy of the church. We are fighting today for costly grace."[18]

But if the cost of discipleship is great, the goal is glorious. Jesus says so, and we cannot fail to remind our listeners of his words in this regard. The same Jesus who bids us "come and die" says: *"whoever loses their life for me will save it"* (Luke 9:24). Bonhoeffer's final sentences in his chapter on "Costly Grace" put it well:

> Happy are they who, knowing that grace, can live in the world without being of it, who, by following Jesus Christ, are so assured of their heavenly citizenship that they are

truly free to live their lives in this world. Happy are they who know that discipleship simply means the life that springs from grace, and that grace simply means discipleship. Happy are they who have become Christians in this sense of the word. For them the word of grace has proved a fount of mercy.[19]

3

PREACHING WHAT JESUS SAYS ABOUT SEX AND MARRIAGE

There are not many topics more difficult to preach than sex and marriage. Several pitfalls await any preacher who preaches on what Jesus says on the subject. For starters, what Jesus proclaimed about sex and marriage differs widely from the values held by twenty-first-century Westerners. Lust seems to be a national pastime, so Jesus' strong words about curbing lust sound out of touch to many listeners. Jesus' words about divorce seem harsh, too, considering how many people in our congregations have experienced divorce in their pasts.

Second, the strong statements Jesus makes about sex and marriage can cause listeners a lot of pain. Every time I preach on a text in which Jesus addresses divorce, I say something like: "I wish I could divide you up into two groups. Some of you have felt the searing pain of divorce, and I do not wish to present Jesus' strong words about it in a way that compounds your pain. But another group needs to hear Jesus' strong words about divorce because you have not experienced the pain and may be considering divorce as an option."

Third, the topic is awkward for the typical congregation of listeners who vary in gender and age. I have no qualms about using terms like *masturbation* or *oral sex* when necessary. But I know that some of my listeners on both the younger and older ends of the spectrum will not hear anything else I say once they hear these words. Not long ago, a mother e-mailed me after I preached a sermon on sex and asked if I would let her family know the next time I preached on issues related to sexuality. She wanted to make sure she took her children elsewhere on that particular Sunday!

Finally, much of what Jesus says about sex and marriage is difficult to interpret. How are we to understand his counsel to gouge out our eyes or cut off our hands in order to curb lust (Matt. 5:27–30)? What are we to make of Jesus' strong statements about "no divorce," particularly when one gospel writer records an exception and another does not (see Matt. 19:9 and Mark 10:11–12)? What do we do with Jesus' statement about eunuchs, and what application does this have to the choice to be single? How do we process Jesus' silence on homosexuality—one of the most explosive topics of our age? Why did Jesus not condemn it if it really is a sin?

Certainly, preaching what Jesus says about sex and marriage is an exceedingly difficult challenge, but we cannot shy away from it. Both the well-being of our listeners and the glory of God are at stake. John Piper rightly declares that "marriage is the *display* of God. It is designed by God to display his glory in a way that no other event or institution does."[1] It is no wonder, then, that the most intimate, ecstatic human relational act—sexual intercourse—is reserved for marriage. According to Proverbs 5:19, the one type of intoxication that is entirely appropriate is intoxication with the love of our spouse. When people stray from the boundaries God has set for using sex, they dishonor him and cause themselves and others great pain (see Prov. 5:1–14, 22–23).

So let's consider how to preach what Jesus says about sex and marriage in a way that promotes the glory of God, the gospel of Jesus Christ, and the good of our listeners. Specifically, we will consider what Jesus says about five topics related to sex and marriage: lust, marriage, divorce, singleness, and homosexuality.

Lust

As I suggested earlier, lust has become our national pastime. I realized how thoroughly lust had sunk its tentacles into the psyche of our culture a few summers ago when the media carried a story about Christie Brinkley's divorce trial. She had filed for divorce against her husband after she learned that he was having an affair with a teenager. According to her testimony, a contributing factor to her husband's behavior was the depth to which he was into pornography. In fact, the two of them would use pornography to get the mood going between them. The irony is that Christie Brinkley is a former *Sports Illustrated* model, a super model, and a sex-symbol in our culture. How tragic. A man married even to a supermodel felt he needed other stimuli for sexual satisfaction, and the dark journey resulted in an affair with a teenager.

Jesus does not get far into his Sermon on the Mount before he addresses the problem of lust. In a section of the Sermon where he is raising the bar regarding the kind of righteousness required for living in God's kingdom, he says:

> You have heard that it was said, "You shall not commit adultery." But I tell you that anyone who looks at a woman lustfully has already committed adultery with her in his heart. If your right eye causes you to stumble, gouge it out and throw

it away. It is better for you to lose one part of your body than for your whole body to be thrown into hell. And if your right hand causes you to stumble, cut it off and throw it away. It is better for you to lose one part of your body than for your whole body to go into hell. (Matt. 5:27–30)

Haddon Robinson is certainly right when he identifies the big idea of this section as: "Adulterous desires corrupt relationships; therefore, we ought to deal with them drastically."[2] But preaching this text and its big idea will require a preacher to address at least two questions that typically trouble listeners. Without reasonable answers, listeners will simply not buy into what Jesus says about lust.

1. What is so bad about lust?
2. How will the actions Jesus suggests really help people stop lusting?

The place to begin is helping our listeners understand what is so bad about lust. When I preached this text recently to the congregation I serve as pastor, I approached this question by first helping them understand what is *not* sinful about lust. For starters, lust is not sinful because it is an intense desire. A person can have an intense desire to serve his country, care for her children, or wipe out crime. The word for lust (*epithumeo*) in Matthew 5:28 simply refers to a desire or a longing, and it is sometimes used positively in other contexts. In fact, in Luke 22:15 Jesus said to his disciples: "I have eagerly desired (*epithumeo*) to eat this Passover with you before I suffer." Yes, it is the same word used negatively and translated *lust* in Matthew 5:28!

Furthermore, lust is not bad because it fantasizes or imagines. You can imagine running on a beach with a cool ocean

42

breeze and the misty spray. You can imagine thunderous applause after you round third base and head for home. You can imagine the wind whipping in your face as you let your horse go full gallop. You can imagine the growth of the church you plant and how it will transform your community. What makes imagination acceptable or sinful is the content of what you imagine.

Nor is lust sinful because it is sexual. We dare not equate sexual desire with the lust Jesus condemns. As texts such as Proverbs 5 indicate, sex is a good gift from God, and it is normal for men and women to be attracted to each other. This reflects the creation of human beings as sexual beings. God created humans as male and female, not as androgynous beings (Gen. 1:27).

Lust is sinful because it is an intense fantasy or desire for sexual relationship outside the boundaries God has established. The playing field for sexual activity is marriage. Sin enters and corrupts God's good gift when our imaginations turn to sexual encounters that are clearly "out of bounds." In a recent sermon on this text, I told my listeners that Jesus is not telling them to be blind to physical beauty—his words on gouging out one's eye notwithstanding! Recognizing physical attractiveness in someone of the opposite sex is not sin. But what happens next will determine whether or not you do sin. If you start taking off that person's clothes in your mind, or if you start thinking about a passionate embrace, that's lust. If you're married and you start fantasizing that someone else in the office is your spouse, you've lusted.

Still, some listeners will think Jesus has come down too harshly on lust by making such absolute statements about it. He minces no words when he says *"anyone* who looks at a woman lustfully has *already* committed adultery with her in his heart" (Matt. 5:28 italics added). Besides, there is a difference between fantasy and the physical act of adultery, right? I tried to help my listeners see the seriousness of lustful thoughts by likening lust to a plot to assassinate the president of the United States. I explained that if you have plotted to assassinate the president, and your plot is exposed, you are guilty. Never mind that you did not commit the deed. You are guilty for planning it. Furthermore, fantasies are not luxuries, because you will do what you rehearse in your mind. Just as murder begins with anger, sexual sin begins with lust. We're fooling ourselves if we deny the connection.

The second question we must answer for our listeners when we preach Matthew 5:27–30 is how the actions Jesus suggests will help people stop lusting. As noted in an earlier chapter, Jesus uses hyperbole to make his point. I said to my listeners, "I know myself well enough to know that I would not be any less lustful if I gouged out my right eye or cut off my right hand as Jesus counsels in Matthew 5:29–30." Then I talk about what drastic steps a Christ-follower might take to avoid lust. A few examples I gave included controlling or limiting both Internet usage and cable television. If necessary, cut them out. This is not being legalistic. It is being sensible. It resembles some of my older friends with heart conditions who will not visit some of my favorite places in Colorado. It's too bad that they miss out on the scenic beauty and grandeur of the mountains and the streams, but they have the sense to know that the altitude of many of these beautiful locations would be detrimental to their health. Walking around a lake at ten thousand feet above sea level could threaten their well-being. Their decision is not legalistic but realistic. They are looking at the big picture and saying, "I will forgo something that can be good because it has the potential to ruin me."

Other applications of Jesus' words include disciplining our eyes to look away from sexually charged images rather than looking intently at them. This includes the members of the opposite sex we see in supermarkets or at high school band concerts. When we fail to restrain our eyes, they become heat-seeking missiles that zero in on certain body parts and lead our imaginations down a ruinous path to destruction.

Before wrapping up a sermon on Matthew 5:27–30, we need to make sure our listeners are clear on how the gospel provides the help and deliverance we need when we are caught in a cycle of lust. Listeners need to understand that lust is a sin that, like any other sin, makes us deserving of hell. This fact should not lead us to despair but to the cross! Our listeners need to hear that through the death and resurrection of Jesus Christ, we have a new source of righteousness. This is not the legalism of the Pharisees (see Matt. 5:20) but a righteousness "which is through faith in Christ—the righteousness that comes from God on the basis of faith" (Phil. 3:9). This provides hope to those who struggle with lust and have had some kind of a sexual train wreck in their past. Through the gospel of Jesus Christ, we have a new source of power (Phil. 1:6; 2:12–13), a new motivation (2 Cor. 5:17), and a new set of passions (Col. 3:1–4). Obviously, this kind of discussion may take a preacher outside the Gospels to other biblical texts. But it is worth grounding what Jesus says about lust in the gospel as it is articulated in the four Gospels and the rest of the New Testament. I want my listeners to know that what Jesus is asking them to do in curbing lust flows out of their relationship with him—not out of the rules-based, try-harder approach of the Pharisees.

Marriage

When it comes to Jesus' statements about marriage, we find them most in contexts where he discusses divorce (Matt.

5:31–32; 19:1–12; Mark 10:1–12; but see also Matt. 22:23–33; Mark 12:18–27; Luke 20:27–40). Yet a close reading of these texts shows that Jesus is really addressing divorce in the context of marriage. God's design for marriage gives shape to everything that Jesus says about divorce, singleness, and, for that matter, the problem of lust.

Perhaps the most significant point we can make to our listeners is that Jesus held the same high view of marriage articulated in Genesis 2:24—the first statement about marriage in the Bible and the grand conclusion to the double account of creation. We can claim this about Jesus because he quotes this passage at the outset of his response to the Pharisee's question about what constitutes lawful divorce (see Matt. 19:3–6).

Preachers can handle this text—whether in Matthew's account or in the parallel in Mark 10:6–9—in one of two ways. One option is to preach a single message on "what Jesus says about marriage" from this saying. Then a second message could concentrate on Jesus' teaching about divorce in the rest of the passage. The other option is to preach the entire unit (Matt. 19:1–12 or Mark 10:1–12), taking both issues together. While I am a fan of preaching larger units so as to help people think through the flow of the Gospels, this is one place where I would feel free to slow down. Marriage is such a critical issue and challenge that we need to drink deeply from the teaching of Jesus on this subject.

At this point, it should also be apparent that preachers could also put together a series titled What Jesus Says about Sex and Marriage and address the five topics that serve as headings in this chapter: lust, marriage, divorce, singleness, and homosexuality.

However you decide to preach Matthew 19:4–6 (or Mark 10:6–9), there are some key themes worth emphasizing. Since Jesus is quoting primarily from Genesis 2:24, you will make the same basic points you would in an exposition on that text. Here, then, is a brief list of ideas I like to highlight when preaching this passage.

1. Marriage was created by God. Jesus opens his response with a reference to the Creator. This shapes everything he says about marriage. He sees marriage as an institution created by God, not a human-made institution. This is clear from the implication Jesus draws from Genesis 2:24. After quoting this text, he offers this challenge: "Therefore what God has joined together, let no one separate" (Matt. 19:6). Here, a wise preacher will help listeners see the implications. If God is the Creator, then he alone has the authority and the wisdom to determine how marriage is supposed to work—including what is lawful in marriage and what is not.

2. Marriage is grounded in the way God created human beings as sexual beings. By prefacing his quote of Genesis 2:24 with a reference to Genesis 1:27 ("that at the beginning the Creator 'made them male and female'"), Jesus makes it clear that marriage flows out of God's design of human beings as male and female. The writer of Genesis makes this clear, too, by prefacing the first statement of the Bible on marriage with the words "for this reason." Jesus simply affirms that connection. This is important because it affirms the goodness of sex and of marriage.

3. Marriage is a union between a man and a woman. Jesus' strong affirmation of heterosexual marriage leaves no room for homosexual marriage. Again, the link Jesus makes between the first statement about marriage in the Bible (Gen. 2:24) and the statement about God creating human beings as sexual beings (Gen. 1:27) makes it quite clear that the institution of marriage flows out of the creation of human beings as male and female. Jesus' understanding of marriage, then, as based on heterosexuality leaves no theological room for the view that marriage between two men or between two women is legitimate.

4. Marriage is an intimate, exclusive union. Three expressions here communicate this idea. The first is "leave." A man will leave his father and mother. In a day when young men typically entered the family business or trade with their fathers, a newly married couple would often live nearby the groom's parents—perhaps in the adjacent tent. This created the temptation for the young groom not to cut the proverbial apron strings from his mother and instead allow his mother or father, or both, to call the shots in his marriage. The bride is not singled out in Genesis 2:24 because there was no temptation for her in a day when she could be living miles from her parents. She simply had little means of connecting with them centuries before air mail, e-mail, Skype, and text messaging. The concern here is not with breaking relational ties but ties of authority. The new bride and groom need to begin their own family unit.

The second expression is "united to his wife." In the Hebrew text of Genesis 2:24, the word *united* means "to cling, cleave to, stick to."[3] Job 38:38 uses the term to refer to dirt clods that "stick together" after it rains. This provides a good picture of marriage. It's not that husband and wife are a couple of dirt clods, but that their relationship involves a fusion.

The third and final expression is "become one flesh." The term *flesh* is used here in its widest sense of human life, so that becoming "one flesh" means becoming a spiritual, moral, intellectual, and physical unity.[4] Married partners do not cease to be individuals, but marriage weaves their lives together in a unique union. The union is also to be an exclusive one. Bruce K. Waltke offers this comment on Genesis 2:24: "God's intention that marriage be monogamous is implied by the complete unity and profound solidarity of the relationship."[5]

5. Marriage is intended to be a permanent union. This is implied in the conclusion Jesus draws from Genesis 2:24: "Therefore what God has joined together, let no one separate" (Matt. 19:6). This becomes the foundation for what Jesus says about divorce (see below). We might help our listeners picture the reasonableness of Jesus' implication by using the illustration of gluing together a couple of boards. Once a bond has been formed, trying to separate them results in splintering and ripping. The result is that both are damaged. The same thing happens when people try to dissolve a marriage.

In addition, this might be a good place to address a question about a troubling statement Jesus makes about marriage in another context. In response to a question by the Sadducees, Jesus says: "At the resurrection people will neither marry nor be given in marriage; they will be like the angels in heaven" (Matt. 22:30). This answer is a bit disturbing. If there is no marriage in our resurrection life, then won't that life be less than what we have now? Will we not enjoy intimacy with our spouses in our lives on the new earth? My sense is that Jesus does not address these questions since the answers to them should be obvious. We will have such a great capacity for intimacy with Christ and each other in our resurrection life that sexual intimacy will no longer be necessary. However, this does not imply a complete discontinuity between the bond we currently have with our spouses on the present earth and the bond we will share with them on the new earth. Some kind of special relationship may well continue even though that marriage will be eclipsed by a much greater intimacy with God and his people.

Divorce

Now we come to the issue that preachers fear preaching more than anything else: divorce. Jesus' words on divorce are hard to preach for two major reasons. First, listeners often have adverse reactions to sermons on divorce even if the preacher handles the text and its big idea well. Whatever a preacher says about the teaching of Jesus on divorce is sure to stir up some combination of anger, guilt, shame, sadness, and even despair. Second, evangelicals who take the Bible seriously differ as to what Jesus meant by what he said about divorce and remarriage. How can pastors preach effectively on this difficult subject regardless of their understanding of what Jesus meant? Both issues must be addressed and handled well.

Let's begin with the interpretation issue. My first introduction to the sharp disagreement among evangelicals over Jesus' understanding of divorce and remarriage came when I read two books on the matter by two of my seminary professors. Both received their master's degrees at the seminary where they taught and I attended. Both received their doctorates in biblical studies from another prominent evangelical seminary. Both taught in the same department as colleagues. Yet their books took entirely different approaches. One professor did not see any legitimate grounds for divorce and remarriage, understanding Jesus' "exception" in Matthew 19:9 to refer to a unique situation within Jewish culture—marriage between near relatives prohibited by Leviticus 18:6–18.[6] The other professor held that Jesus allowed divorce and remarriage when marital unfaithfulness had broken the marriage bond beyond repair.[7] The situation is no different today. Expect to find disagreement among scholars and pastors who work side by side in the same institutions, denominations, and movements.

So what is a preacher to do? To sort through the various exegetical issues and argue my conclusion does not seem to be the most helpful way for me to help you figure out how to preach on the difficult texts that record what Jesus taught about divorce. Besides, this would require a separate book. Instead, let me offer some suggestions as to the key issues to study and the resources to consult. I counsel you to give yourself some time—weeks or months—to research and wrestle with the issue. Unless you have studied this issue before, one week before you preach is not enough time for understanding, sorting through, and arriving at conclusions about what Jesus meant when he taught on divorce. I do not claim that the following list is exhaustive, but these are the key questions you must settle in your mind before you can offer your interpretation.

1. How was Deuteronomy 24:1–4 (raised by the Pharisees in Matthew 19:7 and commented on by Jesus in Matthew 19:9) understood in Judaism at the time of Jesus?

2. What is the meaning of "sexual immorality" (*porneia*) in Jesus' "exception clause" in Matthew 19:9?

3. Why does Jesus' "exception clause" in Matthew 19:9 not appear in the parallel passage in Mark 10:1–12?

4. Do Jesus' exception in Matthew 19:9 and Paul's teaching in 1 Corinthians 7:15 intend to provide the only two instances where divorce and remarriage are permissible, or do they work out a more basic principle in their specific historical circumstances that might be applicable to other circumstances?

The fourth question was raised by Craig L. Blomberg in a thoughtful article on Matthew 19:3–12. He joins other interpreters in wondering if the exceptions raised by Jesus and Paul have application to cases of insanity, extreme alcoholism, drug abuse, and physical abuse.[8]

Other helpful resources include, of course, the major commentaries on the Gospels of Matthew and Mark as well as a recent volume presenting and interacting with the three main evangelical views on divorce and remarriage. The book is titled *Remarriage after Divorce in Today's Church: Three Views* (Zondervan); the editor is Mark L. Strauss. Gordon J. Wenham argues for the "No Remarriage after Divorce" view, William A. Heth for "Remarriage for Adultery or Desertion," and Craig S. Keener for the "Remarriage for Circumstances beyond Adultery or Desertion" view.

When preaching on what Jesus says about divorce a preacher has to deal with a second major issue: the adverse reactions on the part of the listeners. Some are wounded, and the wounds are still raw from their experience of divorce. They may be angry or in despair. Others are hurting from the stigma attached to divorce. They may feel like their divorce makes them second-class citizens in God's kingdom, or they may feel—rightly or wrongly— that their church feels this way about them. As I said at the outset of this chapter, I have told my listeners when preaching on Matthew 19:1–12 or Mark 10:1–12 that I would prefer to divide them up into two groups: those who have been divorced and those who have not. Many of those in the former group need encouragement and help moving ahead with their lives. Those in the second group need the kind of warning that Jesus was offering to the Pharisees when he addressed their question—one that reflected a rather loose view of divorce and remarriage.

Since this is not possible, I try to help all my listeners see the wonderful blend of grace and compassion behind Jesus' stern words. While I have not personally experienced divorce, I try to identify with listeners who have by saying something like, "Those of you who have been divorced understand more than anyone else here today why Jesus said what he did. You have lived through the pain that comes with divorce. You of all people can appreciate that what Jesus is saying does not emerge from a harsh, mean-spirited, narrow-minded perspective. Jesus is speaking out of love. He does not want to see people get hurt, which is what happens when divorce takes place. If Jesus sounds harsh, it is because he wants to prevent people from hurting others. He is talking to a group of leaders who had men in their ranks who thought it was all right to divorce their wives if their wives burned dinner or if they found a different woman more attractive!"[9]

This is such a key point. Jesus is speaking out of grace and compassion for people, not out of a strict, uncaring idealism. It is his grace and compassion that leads to a stern warning to those who are tempted to violate God's design for marriage to fulfill their own desires.

Singleness

While Jesus does not provide a full-orbed theology of singleness, he does broach the subject at the end of his discussion with the Pharisees about divorce. In response to his teaching, his disciples said to him: "If this is the situation between a husband and wife, it is better not to marry" (Matt. 19:10). Jesus offered this reply:

Not everyone can accept this word, but only those to whom it has been given. For there are eunuchs who were born that way, and there are eunuchs who have been made eunuchs by others—and there are those who choose to live like eunuchs for the sake of the kingdom of heaven. The one who can accept this should accept it. (Matt. 19:11–12)

When Jesus says that "not everyone can accept this word," he is most likely referring to the disciples' statement that "it is better not to marry" in light of such a strict view of divorce and remarriage as taught by Jesus. As Grant Osborne points out, Jesus has "made marriage unattractive since they could easily be trapped in an unhappy relationship."[10] Carson understands the disciples' remark to be cynical given the common view that marriage was a duty.[11] Judaism as a whole did not emphasize celibacy, as the community at Qumran did.[12]

Even though the disciples' remark is cynical, Jesus does not brush it off but uses it as an opportunity to provide a brief treatment of singleness. We should keep in mind that his teaching comes immediately after he has articulated a high regard for marriage and has based it on the way God created human beings as sexual beings. This teaching comes, too, from one who is single!

Jesus begins by distinguishing between reasons why men in his culture were single. First, "there are eunuchs who were born that way." Osborne takes this as a description of "those born without sexual organs or impotent."[13] Second, Jesus refers to "eunuchs who have been made eunuchs by others." France explains: "The deliberate castration of men, particularly in order to provide 'safe' attendants of a married woman or custodians of a harem, was widely practiced throughout the ancient world. The practice is known, but not approved in the OT (Isa 56:3–5;

cf. Deut 23:1); specific instances are invariably associated with a pagan court (2 Kgs 9:32; 20:18; Esther passim; Acts 8:27)."[14]

It is Jesus' third category of eunuchs that is striking. He speaks of "those who choose to live like eunuchs for the sake of the kingdom of heaven" (Matt. 19:12). The Greek text literally reads: "who make themselves eunuchs for the sake of the kingdom of heaven." Most interpreters throughout the centuries have understood this as "a metaphor for making the choice to remain unmarried."[15] Jesus obviously sees this approach as a legitimate expression of discipleship. But his closing statement makes it clear that it is not a requirement for all disciples: "The one who can accept this should accept it." Singleness, then, is a "valid calling"—but not a "higher calling"—for those who can accept it.[16] This aligns with Paul's teaching in 1 Corinthians 7:7–9 where he commends celibacy, probably for its ability to free people for more kingdom ministry, but argues that it is better to marry than to burn with passion.

Once again, preachers have a couple of options when it comes to preaching Matthew 19:10–12. One is to preach Jesus' teaching on singleness as a subsection of a sermon that covers Matthew 19:1–12 and addresses the issues of marriage, divorce and remarriage, and singleness. The other option is to preach a lone sermon on Matthew 19:10–12 devoted entirely to the subject of singleness, emphasizing that it is a legitimate—though not required—strategy for giving oneself wholly to the kingdom of God.

Homosexuality

In many respects, handling Jesus' attitude toward homosexuality is the hardest aspect of preaching on what Jesus says about sex and marriage. The reason for this is that Jesus does not address homosexuality by name. The silence is deafening. Those who claim to take the Bible seriously and yet advocate or accept homosexual behavior will typically argue that since Jesus did not condemn homosexuality neither should we. However, we have already seen that Jesus' understanding of marriage is based on God's heterosexual design of human beings and leaves no theological room for the view that marriage between two men or between two women is legitimate. This is a strong argument since it is made from design, not silence.

Furthermore, Jesus is not as silent about homosexuality as people usually assume. New Testament scholar James De Young notes, "Jesus referred to Sodom and its destruction more frequently than did anyone else (Matt. 10:15; 11:23; Luke 17:26–37). In each context, Jesus assumes the divine judgment on Sodom, which He links to the Flood as an example of divine intervention. . . . He views the sin of Sodom as a serious matter."[17] De Young notes that four other references to Sodom occur in the New Testament (Rom. 9:29; 2 Pet. 2:6–11; Jude 1:7; Rev. 11:8) and that both Peter and Jude identify homosexuality as the sin of Sodom.[18] So in reality, Jesus does condemn homosexual practice, though implicitly instead of explicitly. For whatever reason, he was content to condemn homosexual practice with an indirect reference rather than with a specific word against it. Only by pitting the four Gospels against the remainder of the New Testament can one argue that Jesus did not condemn homosexual practice.

As homosexuality becomes a more polarizing issue in our culture, pastors need to learn how to speak firmly and yet graciously about this—condemning homosexual practice along with other sexual sins while holding out the gospel and its grace as the power of God for salvation from this sin's lure and grip.

What New Testament scholar Thomas Schmidt says about Christians in general certainly applies to pastors who address this issue in their preaching: "Christians who cannot yet deal with the issues calmly and compassionately should keep their mouths shut, and they should certainly stay away from the front lines of ministry and public policy debate—not to mention television talk shows."[19] This is not to promote timidity over boldness. But to gain a hearing in our culture, it seems that this is a case where "a gentle tongue can break a bone" (Prov. 25:15). Fiery words will simply cause listeners to quit listening.

Difficult but Necessary

There are not many topics more difficult to preach than sex and marriage. I made this claim at the outset of the chapter. But let me offer a second claim. There are not many topics more needed by your listeners than sex and marriage. Christ-followers regularly get derailed by lust and wrecked by extramarital affairs. To help our listeners and ourselves keep from making junkyards out of our marriages, we will do well to provide careful, thoughtful expositions of the teaching of Jesus on all topics related to sex and marriage.

4

PREACHING WHAT JESUS SAYS ABOUT HELL AND JUDGMENT

O sinner! Consider the fearful danger you are in: 'tis a great furnace of wrath, a wide and bottomless pit, full of the fire of wrath, that you are held over in the hand of that God, whose wrath is provoked and incensed as much against you as against many of the damned in hell: you hang by a slender thread, with the flames of divine wrath flashing about it, and ready every moment to singe it, and burn it asunder; and you have no interest in any mediator, and nothing to lay hold of to save yourself, nothing to keep off the flames of wrath, nothing of your own, nothing that you ever have done, nothing that you can do, to induce God to spare you one moment.[1]

Jonathan Edwards spoke these words in his infamous sermon "Sinners in the Hands of an Angry God." When I read this excerpt, the caricature that comes to mind is an animated preacher who is gesticulating wildly, sweating profusely, and shouting at his listeners. But eyewitnesses reveal that the noise and hysteria that accompanied the sermon was entirely on the part of the listeners—not the preacher. Edwards's biographer George Marsden notes that "Edwards had none of the dramatic gestures of a Whitefield or a Tennent and was said to preach as though he were staring at the bell-rope in the back of the meetinghouse."[2] An eyewitness who heard this sermon preached at Enfield, on the Massachusetts-Connecticut border, described his delivery as "easy, natural and very solemn. He had not a strong, loud voice. . . . he made but little motion of his head or hand in the desk, but spake so as to discover the motion of his own heart."[3] Yet the effect was stunning. People shrieked and cried out. Edwards even stopped his sermon and asked for silence. Yet the wailing continued, so he never finished the sermon. Still, there were several conversions that night of July 8, 1741. Edwards's "terrifying vision" of hell turned out to be "the means God used to bring the joys of salvation."[4]

At the dawn of the twenty-first century, a *U.S. News & World Report* cover story article titled "Hell Hath No Fury" made this insightful, poignant observation: "Edwards would scarcely recognize the hell of today. After decades of near obscurity, the netherworld has taken on a new image: more of a deep funk than a pit of fire."[5] Another decade later, *Time* magazine offered a cover story article titled "Is Hell Dead?" It focused on the latest challenge to Dante's *Inferno* and Edwards's fiery pit—a new image of hell envisioned by Rob Bell, author of *Love Wins*, a book about heaven, hell, and the fate of every person who ever lived. According to the article, Bell and a new generation of thinkers want us to ask whether our idea of hell "is truly rooted in the New Testament or is attributable to subsequent church tradition and theological dogma."[6] This is a fair question, and one that preachers must wrestle with when expounding the texts in the four Gospels that record Jesus' teaching on hell and judgment.

These texts are notoriously difficult to preach given the challenge of understanding them truly and proclaiming them clearly in a culture whose mood makes it difficult for listeners to stomach what Jesus says about hell and judgment. Besides, how much of Jesus' language is metaphorical as opposed to literal? Does Dante's inferno or Edwards's fiery pit or "Bell's hell" reflect what Jesus really taught?

The Fire of Gehenna

Ironically "much of the most graphic language about hell [in the Bible] comes from the Lord Jesus himself."[7] When Jesus spoke of hell, he used a word picture. The term *geenna*, translated *hell* in our English translations, appears in eleven statements made by Jesus.[8] In the first recorded statement of Jesus about hell in Matthew 5:22, Jesus speaks of the "hell (*geenna*) of fire." He does the same in Matthew 18:9. But in the other ten instances, he simply uses the expression "hell" (*geenna*). D. A. Carson's comments on "hell of fire" are helpful:

> The expression . . . comes from the Hebrew *gê'-hinnōm* ("Valley of Hinnom," a ravine south of Jerusalem once associated with the pagan god Moloch and his disgusting rites [2 Ki 23:10; 2 Ch 28:3; 33:6; Jer 7:31; Eze 16:20; 23:37] prohibited by God [Lev 18:21; 20:2–5]). When Josiah abolished the practices, he defiled the valley by making it a dumping ground for filth and the corpses of criminals (2 Ki 23:10). Late traditions suggest that in the first century it may still have been used as a rubbish pit, complete with smoldering fires. The valley came to symbolize the place of eschatological punishment.[9]

This, of course, raises the question as to what extent the language of hell is literal or metaphorical. If the Valley of Hinnom is a symbol, then what is the referent—eschatological punishment—like? To get help with this question I turned to D. A. Carson. In a chapter titled "On Banishing the Lake of Fire," Carson responds to "annihilationists" like John Stott who believe in the destruction of the wicked but not in a conscious, eternal suffering. Carson grants that "there is a substantial metaphorical element in the Bible's descriptions of hell." However, he is adamant that "this does not mean that hell itself is merely metaphorical: one must not infer from the fact that someone thinks that many of the descriptions of hell are metaphorical and not literal the conclusion that hell itself is not literal. Hell is real."[10]

Preachers need to impress those last three words on their listeners when they preach on what Jesus says about hell. *Hell is real.* Admitting that Jesus used metaphor or symbol to describe hell does not soften hell's horror. No, Jesus chose the metaphor precisely for the level of horror it conveys. But exactly how metaphorical is Jesus' language? Our listeners want to know. Is the language completely metaphorical, conveying the horrible, painful suffering that nonbelievers will face apart from the presence of God and the majesty of his power? Or is there a vestige of flames or fire in the place of eternal punishment? Once again, I turned to D. A. Carson for help with this question.

In private correspondence, Carson began by noting some other images used by Jesus and the apostles for hell. In 2 Peter 2:4 and 17, hell is described as a place of "darkness" and "blackest darkness." Jesus himself uses a rather different image than burning toward the end of a parable in Luke 12:47 where he describes disobedient servants as being beaten with many or few blows. Yet Carson was quick to add the following caveat: "Precisely *because* 'fire' language predominates, one should not be too quick to claim it is all 'merely' metaphorical, because some will hear such asseverations to be reducing the severity of hell."[11]

Jesus, of course, uses other words and images. In a warning in Matthew 18:6–9 about causing his "little ones"—that is, disciples—to stumble, Jesus juxtaposes the fate of "eternal fire" (v. 8) and "the fire of hell" (v. 9) with having a large millstone hung around one's neck and being drowned in the depths of the sea (v. 6). The "drowning by millstone" image confirms rather than mitigates the horrors of final judgment. On one occasion, Jesus uses the expression "Hades" (Greek, *hades*). Both Matthew 11:23 and Luke 10:15 record this statement. It appears that Gehenna and Hades were commonly used as synonyms. So again, there is nothing inherent in the term or its usage that softens the horror of the fate to which Jesus refers.

How "Eternal" Is Hell?

This leads to another question that troubles our listeners and that we must address when preaching on what Jesus teaches about hell. The question is, how "eternal" is hell? John Stott surely expresses the emotions of many believers when he confesses:

> I find the concept [of eternal conscious punishment in hell] intolerable and do not understand how people can live with it without either cauterizing their feelings or cracking under the strain. But our emotions are a fluctuating, unreliable guide to truth and must not be exalted to the place of supreme authority in determining it. As a committed Evangelical, my question must be—and is—not what does my heart tell me, but what does God's word say?[12]

Along the same lines, Carson understands why people

> question whether the notion of an eternal hell of conscious torment is *fair*. No matter how grievous the offense, no

matter how wretched the sinner—a Hitler, perhaps—is *eternal* hell appropriate? Searing pain that goes on and on, for billions of years, and then more billions of years, and never stops, because all of those billions of years are as a drop in the ocean?[13]

What exactly does Jesus claim, and how can we proclaim it clearly, accurately, firmly, and compassionately to our listeners? A sermon on a text where Jesus speaks of hell is probably not the place for a full-blown defense of the doctrine of eternal, conscious punishment. However, preachers can and should take the time to make a couple of key points. The first point has to do with Jesus' expression "eternal fire" in Matthew 18:8 and 25:41. While the term *eternal (aiōnion)* properly means *age,* the final age is open-ended. As Carson observes, Matthew can use the term *aiōn* "both in a temporal sense and in an eternal sense in the same verse."[14] In Matthew 12:32, Jesus says: "Anyone who speaks a word against the Son of Man will be forgiven, but anyone who speaks against the Holy Spirit will not be forgiven, either in this age or in the age to come."

A second point has to do with Jesus' teaching on hell in Mark 9:42–48. Here, Jesus describes hell as a place "where the fire never goes out" and as a place "where 'the worms that eat them do not die, and the fire is not quenched.'" The latter description is a quotation from Isaiah 66:24. Although R. T. France says that this passage does not settle the debate as to whether the unquenchable fire refers to the unending conscious torment of its inhabitants or simply to a fire that destroys but never goes out because it continually receives new fuel, he does note a passage from the Old Testament Apocrypha that "clearly understands the victims of worm and fire to remain conscious."[15] The passage is Judith 16:17:

> Woe to the nations that rise up against my people!
> The Lord Almighty will take vengeance on them in the
>   day of judgment;
> he will send fire and worms into their flesh;
>   they shall weep in pain forever. [NRSV]

It is difficult, then, to understand Jesus' teaching on "eternal fire" as anything less than ongoing conscious suffering. But *why* is eternal, conscious punishment necessary? Why not have evildoers simply be destroyed through annihilation? We must be honest with our listeners at this point and emphasize that God has not seen fit to give us a complete answer in Scripture. However, while we must not present conjecture as a definitive answer, we might offer a possible reason to help listeners realize that this doctrine is not unreasonable.

One possible answer lies with the severity of sin. Our sin, even the smallest (in our view) infraction, is a severe, egregious act of rebellion when seen in light of the magnitude of a holy God. Perhaps it is like a halfhearted threat such as "I am going to kill you." When a high schooler says this to a sibling, it may simply warrant a verbal rebuke. But if the same high schooler makes this threat against the president of the United States, it may warrant a jail sentence! Our sin, then, is serious based on the magnitude of the one who is offended.

The problem with this answer, though, is that Jesus recognized levels or degrees of punishment. For example, he said to the residents of Chorazin and Bethsaida: "But I tell you, it will be more bearable for Tyre and Sidon on the day of judgment than for you" (Matt. 11:22). Similarly, he says to Capernaum: "But I tell you that it will be more bearable for Sodom on the day of judgment than for you" (Matt. 11:24). Jesus' words in Luke 12:47–48 about some being beaten with more blows and some with fewer blows also reflects his belief in degrees of punishment. Once we have levels of punishment, we may legitimately wonder how *eternal* punishment makes sense alongside these various levels.

There is another way to make sense of the need for eternal punishment rather than a final, yet limited, punishment like annihilation. Carson offers this proposal: "What is hard to prove, but seems to me probable, is that one reason why the conscious punishment of hell is ongoing is because sin is ongoing."[16] Carson sees a hint of this in the angelic interpreter's words to the apostle John in Revelation 22:11: "Let the one who does wrong continue to do wrong; let the vile person continue to be vile; let the one who does right continue to do right; and let the holy person continue to be holy." Carson recognizes that the primary emphasis in this passage is on the time from now until judgment. "Nevertheless," he continues, "the parallelism is telling. If the holy and those who do right continue to be holy and to do right, *in anticipation of the perfect holiness and rightness to be lived and practiced throughout all eternity*, should we not also conclude that the vile continue their vileness *in anticipation of the vileness they will live and practice throughout all eternity?*"[17]

Pastoral Approaches to Preaching What Jesus Says about Hell

After working through the exegetical and theological issues, and after arriving at our own convictions, we still have the task of proclaiming what Jesus says about hell to our people. This is a daunting task. How can we do this as good pastors who care about Jesus' people and about the lost that he came to seek and to save? Here are three ways to proceed.

1. Preach exactly what Jesus says. Admittedly, this sounds like a given. What preacher of the gospel who takes Scripture seriously would not preach exactly what Jesus says? However, there is a real tendency—and a real danger—in our day to subvert what Jesus says by questioning whether or not we have read Jesus' words correctly. This sounds like the noble approach of the Bereans (see Acts 17:11), but it can become a sneaky way of getting around Jesus' strong words about eternal judgment.

In my view, Rob Bell has done this in his book *Love Wins*. He has evaded the hard sayings of Jesus on hell by raising questions about our understanding of them. Personally, I am all for asking the hard questions, and Bell is a master at framing them. For example, he asks the question I just discussed above: "Does God punish people for thousands of years with infinite, eternal torment for things they did in their finite years of life?"[18] Yet Bell ends up dealing with the question by opting for an understanding of hell as a kind of cover-term for the consequences of failing to live in God's world God's way rather than for final, eternal judgment.[19] How does he arrive at this answer? He does so by planting doubts about whether or not we have understood what Jesus was really saying. On one level, I have no argument with that. In fact, that is what this volume is really about. We must not let our preconceived notions or our misunderstandings or our biases get in the way of understanding what Jesus said and what he meant by what he said. But at another level, we must be willing to accept what Jesus says at face value when we have gone to all possible lengths to understand his message.

One way that Bell sets up his final answer to the question about the meaning of hell is to ask, "Who is Jesus talking to?"[20] Then he spends several paragraphs arguing that "Jesus did not use hell to try and compel 'heathens' and 'pagans' to believe in

God, so they wouldn't burn when they die. He talked about hell to very religious people to warn them about the consequences of straying from their God-given calling and identity to show the world God's love."[21] Agreed. Bell continues: "Jesus talked about hell to the people who considered themselves 'in,' warning them that their hard hearts were putting their 'in-ness' at risk." Exactly. But how does Jesus' warning to people relying on their ethnicity or religious performance about hell lead to the conclusion that his words do not apply to heathens and pagans?

As I survey the passages in the Gospels in which Jesus talks about hell, I notice the wide array of sins that make people deserving of hell. These sins include anger against others (Matt. 5:22), lust (Matt. 5:29), causing other disciples to sin (Matt. 18:5–9), and hypocrisy (Matt. 23:15). If these sins make people deserving of hell, how much more do sins like unbelief, murder, and sexual immorality put people under the same condemnation!

My point here is not to provide a full rebuttal to *Love Wins*. Others have done that. I am simply arguing that our preaching about hell must match the way Jesus preached about it. Jesus' proclamation was direct, bold, firm, unapologetic, and full of vivid imagery. While he did not wear a jacket saying "Turn or Burn" like the protestor Bell lampoons at the beginning of his chapter on hell, Jesus did more than raise questions. To use Bell's language, Jesus used "a loaded, volatile, adequately violent, dramatic, serious word"[22] (*Gehenna*) to describe the final judgment reserved for those who refuse to repent and turn to God. Jesus gives every indication that this is an eternal, conscious punishment. How can we as preachers, then, proclaim something less than this?

2. Acknowledge the pain you and your listeners feel about this doctrine. While we dare not soften the reality of hell, we must preach as those who are pained by the prospect of lost people spending eternity in hell apart from Christ. After pondering and discussing the themes and texts surrounding God's final judgment, Carson writes: "I cannot say I find any of this easy. Even at the brutal level of having relatives and loved ones who have quite openly spurned the gospel, meditation on these texts is painful."[23]

How, then, do we bear this pain? We turn back to the gospel of Jesus Christ, the good news that through the death and resurrection of Jesus, God is at work, graciously seeking lost people and reconciling them to himself. We take comfort in the fact that God is not willing that any should perish (see 2 Pet. 3:9). We continue to hold out the gospel to lost family and loved ones. Then, at those moments when family and friends die without any evidence that they have turned to Jesus, we look to God for comfort. We confess that "weeping may stay for the night, but rejoicing comes in the morning," that we have a God who turns "my wailing into dancing" (Ps. 30:5, 11).

3. Remind listeners that their eternal destinies are at stake. It is easy to lose sight of our aim when we preach on the doctrine of hell. We are speaking to listeners whose eternal destinies hang in the balance. We can overlook this when we focus so much on defending the biblical notion of hell. Or our aversion to the notion of hell can lead us to ignore or obscure its reality. But France is certainly correct when he concludes his comments on Mark 9:43–48 with these sober words:

> This is a matter of ultimate seriousness. Nothing less than eternal life or death is at stake. Christians who disparage "hell-fire preaching" must face that awkward fact that Mark's Jesus (and still Matthew's and Luke's) envisaged an

ultimate separation between life and γέεννα (*geenna*) that demanded the most drastic renunciation in order to avoid the unquenchable fire, and that he did not regard even his disciples as immune from the need to examine themselves and take appropriate action.[24]

France's comment forces me to pause. Throughout my years of ministry, I have not shrunk away from declaring what Jesus says about hell. But I have disparaged "hell-fire preaching." By that, I mean the kind of preaching that, in some traditions, comes across as more of an angry tirade than a loving plea to people. I would argue that our tone matters, and we should avoid coming across as angry or vindictive or cold when proclaiming what Jesus says about hell. Nor should we prey on listeners' emotions. Yet it would be irresponsible not to take the opportunities to sound serious, loving warnings when we come to gospel texts in which Jesus warns listeners about the reality of hell.

Annually the high school from which my son graduated in the north suburbs of Chicagoland prominently displays a wrecked vehicle on the grassy knoll in front of its main entrance. The display coincides with prom when students are more prone to drink and drive. A few parents grouse about how gruesome it is to put a vehicle like this on display. It is too easy to imagine what such a horrific wreck does to its driver and passengers. But this is precisely the point, and most parents are fine with it. They want their students to receive a stern, even shocking, warning to keep them from being maimed or killed in an auto accident. If such a warning strikes fear into teens' hearts and keeps them from such a fate, then the warning and the medium used to convey it is entirely acceptable. And so it is with our preaching on hell. To be sure, the push-back may come from the very people who would support a demolished car on school grounds during prom week. They willingly grant that drinking and driving leads to death in car accidents. What they will not grant is that a life lived in rebellion against God leads to eternal conscious torment. But this does not lessen our responsibility to sound the warning that Jesus gives. The eternal destinies of our listeners are at stake.

Hell and Hope

Hell is a polarizing topic. One group of listeners claims that preachers say too much about it, while the other group argues that preachers say too little about it. Our challenge is to give it the attention Jesus gives to it. When preaching through the Gospels, our responsibility is to unpack with care what Jesus says about hell and judgment.

Ultimately, our challenge when preaching on what Jesus says about hell is to hold out hope. This is why we explain and describe and warn and challenge. We want listeners to turn from a direction that leads them to eternal fire and to pursue Jesus the Messiah, the One through whom they can receive eternal life.

Ironically, when Jonathan Edwards preached his infamous sermon, "Sinners in the Hands of an Angry God" at Enfield, he never finished. As Edwards waited for the wails to subside, they "continued so that there was no way that he might be heard."[25] Yet Edwards's offer of hope did not go unheard. After a closing prayer, the clergy went down among the people to minister to them individually. One of these pastors reported: "Several souls were hopefully wrought upon that night, and oh the cheerfulness and pleasantness of their countenances."[26] That is our reason for preaching boldly and accurately what Jesus says about hell and judgment!

What Marsden says about Edwards's sermon is no less true today when we proclaim what Jesus says about hell: "The seemingly inescapable biblical teaching of eternal punishment, as horrible as Edwards himself found it, could be a wonderful gift if people could be brought to stare into the fire. Only then could they begin to feel its meaning for them. Ironically, that terrifying vision could be the means God used to bring the joys of salvation."[27]

5

PREACHING WHAT JESUS SAYS
ABOUT THE END TIMES

The summer before my second-grade year was a time of anxiety for me. I feared that my teacher might be Mrs. Hovius. I had gotten off to a bad start in my relationship with her toward the end of my first-grade year. Some first-grade classmates and I were amusing ourselves by kicking each other as we sat at our lunch table. All of a sudden, Mrs. Hovius appeared and began scolding us. It seemed like she singled me out. I spent the summer, then, praying that I would get the other second-grade teacher and not Mrs. Hovius. But when the class lists were published about three weeks before the start of school, my worst fears were realized. Mrs. Hovius was going to be my teacher.

On the first day of class, my fears were temporarily relieved when another teacher showed up in class and announced that Mrs. Hovius would be gone on a six-week maternity leave. I had no idea what a maternity leave was, but I rejoiced that I had another six weeks before the teacher I dreaded would return. At the end of six weeks, Mrs. Hovius returned. To make a long story short, she did not live up to any of my preconceived fears. In fact, she remains one of the best teachers I ever had!

My relationship with the teachings of Jesus on the end times resembles my relationship with Mrs. Hovius. It seems like I got off to a bad start with them. As a young teen, I found the Olivet Discourse (Matt. 24–25; Mark 13; Luke 21) particularly frightening. I remember hearing the late musician and evangelist Keith Green preach on the separation of the sheep and the goats in Matthew 25:31–46. His fiery words only reinforced my fear of engaging with this sermon of Jesus. Not only that, I struggled to reconcile Jesus' description of end-time events with the prophecy charts and time lines that were freely distributed in my home church. These suggested a much different experience for the church than for the nation of Israel. Most of the preaching I heard on the Olivet Discourse, aside from Keith Green's message, concentrated on arguing that it did not relate directly to the church today.

Not surprisingly, I harbored a fear about having to preach the Olivet Discourse when, in my second year of pastoral ministry, I decided to preach through the Gospel of Mark. I was apprehensive about arriving at Mark 13. Thanks to my theological training for ministry, I had a more nuanced view of what Jesus taught about the end times. But I knew the people to whom I preached would want a defense of a particular position on eschatology. To my delight, my first foray into preaching the Olivet Discourse left me profoundly touched by the message Jesus was proclaiming. I began to realize that he took the discussion in a different direction as he answered his disciples' questions about when the end-time events would happen and what signs would precede them. He pressed for answers to a more important question about how disciples live in light of the end. The answers satisfied and challenged both me and my listeners.

This chapter will explore how to preach what Jesus says about end-time events regardless of the eschatological view to which you subscribe. There are some basic emphases in what

Jesus teaches about eschatology that transcend your particular views—whether you are amillennial or premillennial, preterist or futurist, or whether you hold to a pre-, mid-, or post-tribulational view of the rapture if you are a premillennialist. These emphases simply cannot be obscured in our preaching if we want to be faithful to the text. Preachers have a golden opportunity to model for our listeners how to focus on Jesus' intent—and that of the four gospel writers—rather than fixating on our own questions and elaborate reconstructions of end-time events.

Going with the Flow

For starters, observe that the Olivet Discourse is simply the climax to what Jesus has to say about end-time events. It is not the first time he broaches this subject. In fact, David L. Turner, in his fine commentary on Matthew, observes: "Eschatology appears in each of Jesus' first four discourses, especially at or near their conclusions (7:22; 10:32, 39–42; 13:49; 18:35), and so it is not surprising that Jesus ends *all* his teaching (26:1) in Matthew with eschatology."[1] Jesus' teaching on the end times is also scattered throughout Luke. It is true that Luke 12:35–48 contains material found in Matthew 24:43–51 and 25:1–13, meaning that Luke simply could have moved it from the Olivet Discourse to another place in his account. However, Bock observes that "much of Luke's unit (12:35–38, 47–48) has no parallel in Matthew, which may show that Jesus taught the parable on multiple occasions."[2] Similarly, the teaching of Jesus in Luke 17:20–37 covers some of the same ground as Luke's account of Jesus' Olivet Discourse in Luke 21:5–36. So it appears that Luke 17:20–37 and 21:5–36 record similar teaching of Jesus on eschatology in two different settings.[3]

The best way to understand what Jesus emphasized when he taught on eschatology is to get a good grasp of the flow of the Olivet Discourse. The following simple outline captures the flow of Matthew's version of what Jesus taught while seated on the Mount of Olives.[4]

I. Jesus' disciples ask two questions (24:1–3).

    A. *When* will this [the destruction of the temple] happen?

    B. *What* will be the sign of your coming and the end of the age?

II. Teaching: Jesus explains what God will do in the future (24:4–35).

    A. Jesus' disciples will experience "the beginning birth pains" between his comings (24:4–14).

    B. Then there will be a time of unprecedented "great distress" (24:15–28).

    C. After this distress, the Son of Man will return with power and great glory (24:29–31).

    D. Jesus' disciples, then, must keep watch for the return of the Son of Man (24:32–35).

III. Application: Jesus exhorts his disciples to let this shape the way they live (24:36–25:46).

    A. Jesus calls them to *alertness* (24:36–25:13).

    B. Jesus calls them to *trustworthiness* (25:14–30).

    C. Jesus calls them to *compassion* (25:31–46).

Wise preachers will keep this structure in front of their listeners, because grasping the flow of a text leads to a better understanding of what ideas the text is communicating. This same flow appears in Mark and Luke, as demonstrated in the chart below. This chart is an adaptation of one presented by Turner in his commentary on Matthew.[5] I have added in italics the parallels—or close variations—that appear out of sequence.

A Brief Synopsis of the Olivet Discourse

Content	Matthew	Mark	Luke
Setting	24:1–3	13:1–4	21:5–7
Beginning of birth pains	24:4–14	13:5–13	21:8–19
Abomination of desolation	24:15–28	13:14–23	21:20–24
Coming of the Son of Man	24:29–31	13:24–27	21:25–27
Lesson of the fig tree	24:32–41	13:28–32	21:28–33
Necessity of alertness	24:42–44	13:33–37	21:34–36
Parable of the servant	24:45–51		*12:41–46*
Parable of the ten virgins	25:1–13		*12:35–38*[6]
Parable of the talents	25:14–30		*19:11–27*
Judgment of the nations	25:31–46		

Now we are ready to explore the key themes emphasized by Jesus when he taught on the end times. Regardless of a preacher's eschatological views, emphasizing these themes is non-negotiable since these are the ones Jesus wanted his listeners to grasp.[7]

Perseverance

The theme with which Jesus begins his Olivet Discourse is perseverance. As already noted, Jesus' answer to the disciples' questions reveals that his concerns about the end times were a bit different than their concerns. His disciples want to know *when* the end-time events would happen and *what* signs would precede them. But Jesus chooses to focus on *how* his disciples should live in light of the end. Jesus' overriding concern in the first part of his discourse is for them to stand firm to the end (Matt. 24:13; Mark 13:13; Luke 21:19).

For the disciples to stand firm and persevere to the end, their first order of business is to avoid deception. They must not be deceived by false messiahs, and they must not be deceived by signs that are simply "the beginning of birth pains" (Matt. 24:8) rather than signs of the end of the age. This second lesson is particularly applicable to the church today. It seems that every time conflict breaks out in the Middle East or an earthquake hits somewhere around the globe, prophecy pundits are quick to say that the end is probably here. To be sure, only a few are foolish enough to set dates for the return of Christ and the end of the world. Most recently, a radio preacher, Harold Camping, proclaimed that Jesus would return on May 21, 2011, and that the world would be destroyed on October 21, 2011—after five months of fire, brimstone, and plagues. But even less radical types come dangerously close to confusing "birth pains" with actual signs of Christ's return when they say that this war or that earthquake is likely an indicator that the end is near. When the first Persian Gulf War began in August 1990, I remember hearing prominent evangelical televangelists say that "while we don't know the date or the hour of Christ's return, the end must certainly be here." Thoughtful preachers, then, will emphasize that national disasters and global catastrophes are "the beginning of birth pains," not necessarily a sign that the end is near.

The title of a recent book by Tim LaHaye and Jerry B. Jenkins raises a question that people in our churches frequently ask. The title of their book is *Are We Living in the End Times?* Unfortunately, in my view, the authors base their answer on both Scripture and current events. My response to this question is always: "Of course we are living in the end times." But my reason why is usually not what people expect. I typically say, "I know that we are living in the last days because the Bible tells me so—not because of the conflict in the Middle East or the rise of national disasters or because of the development of satellite links that could broadcast the two witnesses of Revelation 11 to the entire world."

The reason I am confident we are living in the last times is because of what Hebrews 1:2 says: "In these last days he [God] has spoken to us by his Son." Similarly, 1 Peter 1:20 claims: "He [Christ] was chosen before the creation of the world, but was revealed in these last times for your sake." Likewise, 1 John 2:18 says: "Dear children, this is the last hour; and as you have heard that the antichrist is coming, even now many antichrists have come. This is how we know it is the last hour." The end times or last days, then, refer to the period of time between Christ's first and second comings.

In Jesus' reply to his disciples' questions, it is clear he is more concerned about his disciples' perseverance in preaching the gospel (see Matt. 24:9–11) than about them pinpointing when the end will come. Even premillennialists who hold to a pre-tribulation rapture view grant that "Matthew 24:4–14 summarizes the difficulties the church will face in the early days before 70 A.D. and throughout its existence"[8]—regardless of whether the church is present or not during the Great Tribulation described in Matthew 24:15–28. We have simply not preached Matthew 24:1–14 well if we have not raised the question "how then shall we live?" in response to wars, rumors of wars, famines, and earthquakes. Turner summarizes the answer Jesus gives: "The response of authentic disciples to all these horrifying circumstances is fidelity. Perseverance in obeying Jesus contrasts with lawlessness as the mark of discipleship."[9]

Alertness

Another key theme—and one that is developed at length in the application section of Jesus' Olivet Discourse—is alertness or watchfulness. This theme surfaces as early as Matthew 24:4 when Jesus challenges his disciples: "Watch out (Greek, *blepo*; see) that no one deceives you." It reappears in Matthew 24:32 when Jesus follows up his description of his return with the lesson from the fig tree. Just as the appearance of leaves on a fig tree signal that summer is near, "when you see all these things, you know that it [the return of Christ] is near, right at the door" (24:33).

The full development of this theme comes, though, in 24:36–25:13—at the very beginning of Jesus' "paraenetic" or application section. Turner explains: "At this point, Jesus moves from speaking predictively to speaking paraenetically. From now on, his goal is not to provide additional information to answer the disciples' questions (24:3) but to exhort them on the proper response to that information. This may not be what the disciples want to know, but it is what they need to know."[10]

Jesus' exhortation to alertness lies in 24:36–25:13, a section consisting of two major parts. The first part (24:36–42) is not a parable per se, yet uses parabolic comparisons. The second part (25:1–13) consists of the parable of the ten virgins. Throughout this section, Jesus is adamant that no one knows the day or the hour when the Lord will return (24:36, 42, 44). Life will go on as usual, just as it did in the days of Noah right before the flood (24:38, 40, 41). Then, just as the flood arrived suddenly and unexpectedly, so will the return of the Son of Man (24:39).

The proper response to the unknown and sudden time of Christ's return is to "keep watch" (24:42, 43; Greek, *gregoreo*: keep awake, be alert) and "be ready" (24:44; Greek, *hetoimoi*: be ready, prepared). It is worth spending a couple minutes of a sermon to paint a good word picture of alertness. The best way to do this is to work with Jesus' image of a thief in the night (24:43). When I have preached this text in the past, or its counterpart in Luke 12:39, I have tried to imprint this image on my listeners by presenting it like this:

> I cannot think of many things more traumatic, more horrifying, than having your home burglarized. It is shocking because, in most cases, it is completely unexpected. The thief or thieves come unannounced. There is no phone call saying, "This is the Theft Hotline. A robbery has been scheduled for your house on Wednesday at 2:30 a.m. This is a public service message designed to help you protect your home from this attempt." If you had access to this kind of information, you would keep alert and would take preventative measures to foil the robbery. You would be ready for the arrival of the thief. Since you do not know when you might be robbed, you have to stay alert. That's how it is with Jesus' return. Since you have no idea at what hour he will arrive, you need to keep watch and stay on the alert.

The parable of the ten virgins in Matthew 25:1–13 provides another powerful image of the need for alertness. The parable revolves around ten virgins who are waiting for the wedding procession. In our day, the focus of the wedding procession is the bride as she walks up the aisle to be united in marriage with the groom. But in Jesus' day, no one waited in anticipation for the first chords of "Here Comes the Bride." They waited for the groom to come walking down the street so that they could join the entourage and make their way to the bride's home. The bride, who was beautifully adorned for her husband, was then escorted to the groom's home where a wedding feast was served.[11] In Jesus' parable, the door to the groom's house was shut once the wedding party was inside, presumably to keep out "party crashers" who had no connection to the wedding party but saw this as an opportunity to get free food and drink.

The key detail in the parable, though, concerns the actions of the wise virgins versus the actions of the foolish virgins. The five wise virgins took along oil for their lamps, while the five foolish virgins did not. This detail will require some explanation to contemporary listeners who live in a world lit up by electric or battery-powered lights. Whether the lamps were torches—sticks with oil-soaked rags—or small hand-held clay lamps with wicks, the lamps depended on olive oil for fuel. The five wise virgins bring jars with oil, while the foolish do not. As the result of the bridegroom's delay, the ten virgins fall asleep. When the groom arrived at midnight, the virgins all woke to trim their lamps and join the procession. But the foolish virgins discovered their lamps were almost out of oil. So they ended up searching for a supplier to purchase more. By the time they made their way back, the wedding procession had arrived at the house where the feast would take place. The wedding party was inside, the door was shut, and the five foolish virgins were not admitted.

Jesus provides the punch line to this parable in Matthew 25:13: "Therefore keep watch [*gregoreo*], because you do not know the day or the hour." Jesus' statements in 24:36 and 25:13 about not knowing the day or the hour provide a kind of inclusion, or brackets, around the entire section. So do the exhortations to "keep watch" in 24:42 and 25:13. For Jesus' disciples, then, eschatology motivates alertness. Not knowing when Jesus will return—and knowing that he will return at an unexpected time—should lead Jesus' disciples to be alert to his return. Living as if Jesus might return today will certainly shape our priorities, words, and actions.

We will help our listeners if we can provide some present-day examples or images of alertness. I might liken the kind of alert living Jesus desires to the alertness I have when driving through the school zone near my home as grade schoolers are on their way to school. I have both hands on the wheel, my foot is poised to switch from the gas pedal to the brake, and my eyes are scanning the area immediately in front of me so that I can spot and react instantly to a child who darts out from behind a parked car to cross the street or retrieve a playground ball. I might also liken this alertness to that of a trader watching the stock market, a homeowner who hopes to refinance keeping an eye on interest rates, or a college student paying attention to airline deals for a flight home over the holidays.

Here is a possible sermon outline for Matthew 25:1–13. The main points, or movements, of the sermon are structured around the characters in the parable. The final point is the sermon's big idea.

I. From the bridegroom, we learn that Jesus' return will occur at a time no one can predict.

II. From the foolish bridesmaids, we learn that a lack of preparation for Jesus' return is fatal.

III. From the wise bridesmaids, we learn that *Jesus' followers must stay alert to be ready for the unpredictable timing of his return.*

In the remainder of the Olivet Discourse, Jesus emphasizes two more themes. Alertness is not an end in itself. Alertness means that disciples are so watchful for the return of Jesus that they engage in the kind of service that he wants to see in them when he returns.

Trustworthiness

The first kind of behavior that alertness fosters is trustworthiness or stewardship. Jesus stresses this in his parable of the talents in Matthew 25:14–30. As Turner observes, "The issue here is not whether the slaves will be surprised by the master's return but whether they will be dependable in using his resources. His gifts define their tasks." Furthermore, "The three servants stand for the church, which is once again portrayed as a mixed community."[12] This is an important point. In this parable, Jesus contrasts believers and nonbelievers—those who are his true followers and those who are not. Throughout the Olivet Discourse, Jesus has been discussing the issue of final judgment. So in this parable, those who do not do anything with the resources God has given them, like the third servant who received one talent, are the nonbelievers who are consigned to punishment. Those who wisely invest their resources for the kingdom, like the first two servants who received ten and five talents respectively, are the believers whom God commends.

The key aspect of this parable, I suggest, is how it portrays faithfulness. The master offers both the first and second servants the same commendation: "Well done, good and faithful servant!" (25:21, 23). The term *faithful* (Greek, *pistos*; trustworthy, reliable) is the same term used in 1 Corinthians 4:2 where the apostle Paul writes: "Now it is required that those who have been given a trust must prove faithful." The problem is that faithfulness has often been equated by Christians with playing it safe as opposed to taking bold steps. In the past I have heard church members say about a particularly bold ministry venture our church was about to take: "Let's not take such a risk. God simply calls us to be faithful."

What strikes me about the parable of the talent, though, is how faithfulness involves risk! The doubling of resources involved an investment, and investment involves risk. This parable does not explain the risks these servants took to invest their original capital; the issue here is not technique but attitude. But when we preach this parable, we will do our listeners a service if we help them think through the various kinds of "capital" that God has given them. The examples are endless: musical ability, the capacity to learn new languages, a beach house, athletic ability, a strategic position in a university or in the federal government. In light of Jesus' return, what are we doing with the resources God has given us?

Compassion

The final section of Jesus' Olivet Discourse specifies a second kind of behavior that flows from alertness. The behavior is compassion, expressed in giving thirsty people something to drink, giving needy people clothes to wear, and giving sick and imprisoned people the care and attention they require for their well-being. In light of Jesus' return and the final judgment, Jesus' followers must pay attention to the way they treat "the least of these brothers and sisters" of Jesus (25:40, 45).

The interpretive *crux* of this parable is the identification of the group Jesus describes as "the least of these brothers and sisters of mine." I have heard pastors and commencement speakers use this parable to challenge believers to minister to the world's starving, oppressed, and marginalized. They typically claim: "When you visit the inmates in the county jail, you have visited Jesus. When you give food to an orphan on the streets of Port-au-Prince, Haiti, you have given food to Jesus. When you care for a sick widow or widower in the low-income housing project, you have cared for Jesus." All of these behaviors, of course, are in line with the gospel of Jesus Christ. But we must be careful, here, not to preach the right doctrine from the wrong text.

The "least of these" in Matthew 25:31–46 refers to Jesus' followers—"the community that embodies and extends the message of Jesus."[13] The major evangelical commentators all agree with this.[14] When I have preached this text, I have said it like this: Jesus' followers are all "missionaries" who spread the gospel in the face of hunger, thirst, sickness, and imprisonment. Our response to these missionaries provides the evidence or confirmation of where we will spend eternity. I. Howard Marshall says that the point of this text is that "service to the king's people is service to the king."[15] I find this a helpful way of framing the big idea whenever I preach this text.

The concern over whether this text teaches a form of works-righteousness disappears when we note the surprise of those who are invited into eternal life. They are not performing a certain way to gain eternal life. Rather, their actions function, unknown to them, as a test that reveals their true status and destiny.

So what does it look like for twenty-first-century believers to live out Jesus' call to help out the least of his brothers and sisters? Wise preachers will help their listeners imagine what this looks like in the life of the church. It means visiting sick believers in the hospital or at home. It means spending hours with Christ-followers who are grieving, struggling with depression, or feeling lonely. It may mean opening our home to a young lady who desperately wants to serve Christ but is too distraught to live alone after learning that her fiancé has cheated on her. It means caring for career missionaries.

Our church family just invested dozens of hours and thousands of dollars helping an African pastor and his family return to Kenya after completing a graduate degree here in the United States. His program and living expenses wiped out the reserve he had hoped to use to return home.

A mentor and close friend of mine modeled obedience to this text when he and his wife opened up their home to a young believer in her early twenties who had suffered years of abuse and involvement in satanic rituals. My friend used to sit by her bed during nightmares that lasted as long as two or three hours, reassuring her that Jesus loved her. Jesus says, "You did that for me." Yes, when you serve the king's people, you serve the king. When you serve the king's people, you demonstrate that you belong to the king!

Your Eschatology Is Showing

Preachers need not fear preaching what Jesus said about the end times because of the pressure to explain all the intricate details of when and how Jesus will return. That is not our task. Rather, our task is to challenge people how to live in light of his coming. Eugene Peterson observes: "Eschatology is the most pastoral of all the theological perspectives, showing how the ending impinges on the present in such ways that the truth of the gospel is verified in life 'in the middle.'"[16]

So preach without fear of getting mired in debates over the timing of events and the various millennial views. Preach what Jesus emphasized: the need for perseverance and alertness that leads to trustworthiness as stewards and compassion for fellow "missionaries." This is how Jesus calls us to live in light of his second coming.

6

PREACHING WHAT JESUS SAYS ABOUT GOD'S SOVEREIGNTY AND HUMAN FREEDOM

When preaching the Gospels, it does not take a preacher long to run into texts that contribute to a major theological divide—the divide between Calvinists and Arminians. As early as the prologue of John's Gospel (1:1–14), the tension between God's sovereignty and human ability shows up. It is possible to miss this because the headline in this prologue is, of course, the incarnation. But the tension is there. In John 1:4, the Evangelist reports: "In him [the Word] was life, and that life was the light of all mankind." A few sentences later, John 1:9 says: "The true light that gives light to everyone was coming into the world."

A preacher with a more Arminian bent will see these statements as an expression of prevenient grace, that is, the "grace that precedes and enables the first stirrings of a good will toward God."[1] It is precisely this gift, an Arminian pastor will say, that enables a person to exercise free will in deciding whether or not to accept or reject Jesus Christ as the Evangelist describes it in John 1:11–12.

A preacher with a more Calvinistic bent will argue that a person's decision to believe is predicated upon his or her being born of God (John 1:13). The Calvinist will not see a chronological progression in John 1:12–13 in which belief gives the person receiving Christ the right to become a child of God which then leads to being born of God. Rather, the Calvinist sees the rebirth in verse 13 as the basis for the reception and belief in verse 12. As far as John 1:9 is concerned, the Calvinistic preacher will either view the gift of light to everyone as general revelation, following Calvin himself, or as an objective revelation that ends up dividing the human race.[2] Besides, the "Calvinist's revenge" will come in John 6:44 when Jesus says: "No one can come to me unless the Father who sent me draws them."

But the Arminian preacher will counter by saying, "Yes, no one comes to the Father without being drawn by him, and the Father has done that by serving as "the light of all mankind" (John 1:4) and by giving light to everyone (John 1:9). The argument would continue, of course, with each pastor citing an ever-widening circle of biblical texts both inside and outside of the Gospels. If I wanted to summarize the direction and flow of the argument, it would take me several more pages. At the end of these pages, we would simply reach an impasse!

So what is a preacher to do? My point in this chapter is not to convince you to preach from a Calvinistic perspective or an Arminian perspective. Rather, I want to explore how to preach the texts that expose the Calvinist-Arminian divide in a way that is faithful to the text, regardless of which theological position a preacher holds. How does the proclamation of the four Gospels fundamentally change depending on which side of the line a preacher falls? Furthermore, to what extent should preachers' theological bent shape their reading of a text? Should preachers try to deflect the Calvinist-Arminian issues that surface, or should we take the opportunity to show how our theological system governs the way we understand and apply these texts?

Placing My Theological Cards on the Table

Before I proceed, I want to lay my theological cards on the table. I am a Calvinist. More specifically, I am a moderate Calvinist. This means some of my friends will not find my Calvinism to be Calvinistic enough. For my part, I think some of them have "out-Calvined" John Calvin himself! I think I can be fair when I say this since I am reading through Calvin's *Institutes of the Christian Religion* this year even as I am writing this manuscript. For the record, I do not hold to double predestination. Nor do I hold to limited atonement. I do not object to limited atonement from a "systemic" point of view since, as a Calvinist, I find limitation in election. However, while texts like Matthew 1:21 and Titus 2:14 support the limited or definite atonement view, texts like John 3:16 and 1 John 2:2 widen the scope of the atonement to the "world." I concur with D. A. Carson who writes: "Surely it is best not to introduce disjunctions where God himself has not introduced them. If one holds that the Atonement is sufficient for all and effective for the elect, then both sets of texts and concerns are accommodated."[3] This, I suppose, makes me a "4.5-point" Calvinist.

But if some of my friends find my Calvinism to be less robust than they desire, others find me too Calvinistic for their Arminian tastes. One friend, in fact, recently called me a "hyper-Calvinist." Ironically, the person who rose to my defense was an Arminian! Personally, I reserve the epithet "hyper-Calvinist" for those on the extreme edges whose theology lessens their engagement in evangelism and missions for fear that they may tell a nonelect person that God loves them. In the past, I have challenged such types to read J. I. Packer's *Evangelism and the Sovereignty of God*. Packer writes "to dispel the suspicion . . . that faith in the absolute sovereignty of God hinders a full recognition and acceptance of evangelistic responsibility, and to show that, on the contrary, only this faith can give Christians the strength that they need to fulfill their evangelistic task."[4]

I currently serve in a denomination, the Evangelical Free Church of America (EFCA), that embraces both Calvinists and Arminians.[5] I have no gripes with confessional churches whose statements of faith align themselves with one side of the debate or the other. For example, my friends in the Orthodox Presbyterian Church (OPC) adhere to the Westminster Standards and thus place themselves firmly in the Reformed or Calvinistic stream of theology. My friends in the Church of the Nazarene hold to Articles of Faith that clearly advocate an Arminian view of sovereignty and soteriology. I respect the decision of both groups to make their Calvinistic or Arminian views part of their theological distinctives even as I belong to a movement—the EFCA—that does not. Perhaps both approaches are needed in the current expression of the kingdom of God since both approaches have strengths and weaknesses that I will not explore since they are beyond the scope of this chapter. My preference, though, is to belong to a movement that is rigorously biblical and yet chooses not to make dividing lines out of specific conceptions of tension between God's sovereignty and human responsibility.

Like any conviction, mine has been shaped in part by my background. I have both an Arminian and a Calvinistic heritage. My maternal grandfather, Ernest Zechman, was a lay evangelist in the Susquehanna River valley of Pennsylvania. He worked at a textile mill by day, farmed a bit in the late afternoons and on Saturdays, and then preached at camp meetings in the evenings. He was a staunch Wesleyan Arminian. At his funeral, someone referred to him as the Billy Graham of Snyder County. My paternal grandfather, Leonard Mathewson, was a Baptist pastor who served churches in Pennsylvania and New York State. Even when he retired to the home he built in McKean County in northern Pennsylvania, he continued preaching for two decades until a series of ministrokes ended his preaching ministry. He was a moderate Calvinist, although there was nothing moderate about his passion for eternal security. I possess three or four sermon manuscripts or sermon notes from each of my grandfathers. Not surprisingly, one of the manuscripts by my Arminian grandfather cites Charles Finney approvingly. Meanwhile, notes on one of my Calvinistic grandfather's sermons quote favorably from Augustine. Looking back, it was no small matter for my mother to marry into a family that held to the eternal security of the believer.

I place my cards on the table to show, I trust, that while I write as a Calvinist, I have respect for pastors and scholars in both the Arminian and Calvinist streams of theology. Also, I want to make it clear that I am very aware of the issues that divide and even result at times in divisive Christians. This makes the current chapter even more necessary since pastors throughout North America speak every Sunday to congregations composed of Calvinists, Arminians, and those who are unsure or unaware of the camp to which they belong.

Advice from an Arminian New Testament Scholar

How then should pastors preach texts that expose the divide between Calvinists and Arminians? To get help with this question, I invited to lunch a leading New Testament scholar who happens to be an Arminian. Grant Osborne has been a professor of New Testament at Trinity Evangelical Divinity School for more than thirty-five years. He earned his Ph.D. at the University of Aberdeen under I. Howard Marshall, one of the giants in evangelical New Testament scholarship in the past few decades and himself an Arminian. Osborne is also a fine preacher whose ministry takes him to churches around the Chicago area, even around the world. When we met for lunch, Osborne was getting ready for another trip to Hong Kong to preach and teach the Scriptures.

When I asked Osborne about how his Arminian theology shapes the way he preaches texts from the Gospels, his first words were "I honestly believe that my Arminian position does not change the way I preach the text. I try to bring out the writer's emphasis rather than the whole Arminianism-Calvinism debate."[6] Osborne continued: "I think God wants us to wrestle with the whole issue of God's sovereignty and human responsibility. I want believers to feel secure in Christ, but I am also aware that God calls people to make choices." Lest his remarks be misunderstood, Osborne clarified: "I'm not saying that a preacher has to be a 'Calminian,' but let's allow the text and not our system to decide what we say."

This approach sounds good, especially over lunch, but is it realistic? And if it is realistic, what does it look like in an actual text like John 6:37–44? Osborne was quick to point out that another well-known New Testament scholar, Moises Silva, takes the opposite view. In a book coauthored with Walter C. Kaiser, Jr., *Introduction to Biblical Hermeneutics*, Silva contributed a chapter titled "The Case for Calvinistic Hermeneutics." I am quite sure that Silva's approach is not unique to Calvinists, because I have an Arminian pastor-friend who sides with Silva and not Osborne on this issue. My friend is a pastor, professor, and Ph.D. student in New Testament whose views on this issue are strong enough to make him worthy to write an essay on "The Case for Arminian Hermeneutics."

What, then, is Silva's approach? He writes: "To put it in the most shocking way possible: my theological system should tell me how to exegete. Can such an outrageous position be defended? Three considerations make that position not merely defensible but indeed the only real option."[7] Here is a summary of Silva's three considerations:[8]

1. Systematic theology is largely an exercise in contextualization, that is, the attempt to reformulate the teaching of Scripture in ways that are meaningful and understandable to us in our present context. The very process of organizing the biblical data—to say nothing of the use of a different language in a different cultural setting—brings to bear the theologian's own context.

2. Our evangelical view of the unity of Scripture demands that we see the whole Bible as the context of any one part. Restricting the principle of "the analogy of faith" to the end of the interpretive process—and then only as a means of summarizing the teaching of the passage—amounts to a neglect of God's most important hermeneutical gift, namely, the unity and wholeness of Scripture.

3. Whether we mean to or not, and where we like it or not, all of us read the text as interpreted by our theological presuppositions. The view that exegesis should be done independently of systematic theology is hopelessly naïve.

Silva's points have a lot of merit, and I find myself in general agreement with them. However, they seem to oversimplify the interpretive process. The question is not *whether* we allow our theological system to shape our view of the text but *when* we allow it to shape our view of the text. After talking with Grant Osborne, I am quite confident that he would not argue that our theological presuppositions do not shape our view of the text. In fact, in Osborne's own textbook on hermeneutics, *The Hermeneutical Spiral*, he argues for "the analogy of Scripture" as a controlling principle in interpretation. He recognizes the classic dictum of Milton Terry that "no single statement or obscure passage of one book can be allowed to set aside a doctrine which is clearly established by many passages."[9] Clearly Osborne is not arguing that we can approach the text with a theological "blank slate." But what he does argue for is a process in which the exegetical aspect precedes the process of contextualization and theological formulation.[10]

My sense is that Osborne wants to do the same in preaching. He wants preachers to wrestle with and proclaim what a text says before they show how it fits into the particular theological system to which they hold. I once heard Duane Litfin counsel students in a doctoral seminar on preaching to structure their sermons by taking their listeners over the same set of tracks left in their own study of a passage. In other words, guide your listeners along the contours of the process you followed in wrestling with the text and arriving at an understanding of it. If we do this with texts that expose the debate between Calvinists and Arminians, we might just model for our listeners the way to handle Scripture as we wrestle with matters of God's sovereign choice and human responsibility.

It's All in How You Time It

The issue, then, is one of timing. Preachers do not need to shy away from their theological convictions when preaching texts that expose the issues that divide Arminians and Calvinists. But they must not rush too quickly to these issues at the risk of minimizing the emphasis of a text.

Grant Osborne cites some texts in the Gospel of John as examples. In fact, he feels that the tension between Arminianism and Calvinism is more pronounced in John's Gospel than in the Gospels penned by Matthew, Mark, and Luke. For example, John 6:44 records Jesus as saying: "No one can come to me unless the Father who sent me draws them, and I will raise them up at the last day." When I asked Osborne about this text, he said: "I can agree with John 6:44 as an Arminian! When I preach it, I preach God's eternal choice. I do not get into my 'however,' since foreknowledge is not in the text. I want to stress what this passage does, namely how special we are and how much our salvation is dependent on God's choice of us."

Where, then, should one's theology—whether Arminian or Calvinistic—show up in preaching? For Osborne, this will come in another text at another time. He says: "When I get to John 15, then I stress the seriousness of the warning. I emphasize that we need to persevere and to remain in Christ. I have a problem with preachers on both sides of the spectrum who destroy the intent of the text. Arminian preachers, if they are not careful, can obscure the emphasis on security in John 6, while Calvinist preachers can obscure the emphasis on perseverance in John 15."

A few years ago, I preached through John's Gospel and preached one sermon on John 6—yes, the entire chapter! In the course of this sermon, I chose not to comment at length on

Jesus' statement in verse 44: "No one can come to me unless the Father who sent me draws them." I was not trying to duck the Calvinist-Arminian debate out of fear of stirring up dissent; rather, I felt I had a bigger fish to fry in this passage. My aim was to proclaim the heart of Jesus' message in Capernaum (vv. 25–59), which brought into sharp focus the meaning of the feeding of the five thousand (vv. 1–15) and the deliverance at sea (vv. 16–24). The main idea of my sermon was that *you can satisfy the deepest hunger of your soul only through an intimate relationship with Jesus.* This sets up listeners for the call to respond one way or the other (vv. 60–71). So with seventy-one verses of text to cover in a single sermon, this was not the place to dig into the tension between God's sovereign choice and human responsibility to respond.

If I were preaching a sermon solely on John 6:25–59, I would devote some time to this tension. I would likely follow the lead of D. A. Carson. Even before arriving at Jesus' climactic statement in John 6:44, Carson points out how the tension surfaces in verses 37–40. In verse 37, Jesus says: "All those the Father gives me will come to me, and whoever comes to me I will never drive away." In a popular-level exposition of John 6:37–40, Carson says this about verse 37: "This means, on the one hand, that all of the elect, all of God's chosen people, are viewed as a gift the Father presents to the Son, and, on the other, that once they have been given to Jesus, Jesus for his part will certainly keep them in: he will never drive them away."[11] After reading through verses 38–39, Carson observes:

> Thus God is seen as so sovereign in the process of salvation that the people of God are said to be given as a gift by the Father to the Son, while the Son preserves them to the last day when (he promises) he will raise them up. Nevertheless,

this does not make these privileged people automata. The next verse can describe these same people in terms of what they do.[12]

John 6:40 says: "For my Father's will is that everyone who looks to the Son and believes in him shall have eternal life, and I will raise them up at the last day."

At this point in his exposition, Carson does not probe the mystery or the tension. He simply says: "Both of our propositions are assumed to be true, and neither is allowed to diminish the other."[13] This is often the best course of action. Leave the tension in people's hearts and minds just as the Scripture does. In my experience, people do not like tension and mystery. We want to figure out the details and achieve precision and complete clarity in our understanding. We want to press the tension until everything makes perfect sense to us. But it is worth pointing out to our listeners, as well as to ourselves, that the Bible makes affirmations that seem at odds with each other, yet are both affirmed as true. We can probe these mysteries, but we must accept that our limited knowledge in the present will not allow us to get to the bottom of every mystery.

So a key lesson is to look at the immediate context to see if the balancing factor in the tension is present. If a particular statement lands squarely either on God's sovereignty or on human responsibility, look at the immediate context to see if another statement mitigates this.

Probing the Depths of the Mystery

There are times, though, when we may feel it is appropriate to dig a bit deeper into the mystery. I would do this only if the

Calvinist-Arminian issues have been a topic of debate or concern in the congregation. Here I would tread cautiously and preface my thoughts with the comments I made in the above paragraph regarding the need to live with tension and mystery. Then, as a Calvinist, I would share my reasons why I see God's sovereign election as prior to human responsibility and as unaffected by it. I would share my conviction that foreknowledge is not simply knowing beforehand but choosing beforehand. I would also share my observation that election surfaces predominantly in contexts where the Bible wants to emphasize how much God loves me and how secure I am in his love. I would share my conviction that election never diminishes my responsibility to respond in faith and to share the gospel with others.[14] My Arminian friends would use this as an opportunity to affirm a view of divine sovereignty that understands God's choice to be based on his prior knowledge of how people will respond to the gospel.

Whatever position you take, whether Calvinistic or Arminian, here are some guidelines to follow when you feel compelled to talk about the divide exposed by a particular text in the Gospels.

1. Be careful about labels. Because the terms *Arminian* and *Calvinist* are emotionally charged terms, I usually avoid them in my sermons and instead refer to those who put the emphasis on human freedom and responsibility as opposed to those who believe that God's foreknowledge is prior choice rather than prior knowledge on which he bases his choice to elect some and not others.

2. Represent the other position fairly and accurately. This should be a given in any debate, but the emotions stirred by the Arminian-Calvinist debate often lead to inflamed rhetoric that overstates or misstates the opposing view. Here Calvinistic preachers will do well to consult a source like Roger E. Olson's *Arminian Theology: Myths and Realities*. Arminian preachers will do well to consult Wayne Grudem's *Systematic Theology*. We do the gospel and the cause of Christ a disservice when we misrepresent the views of those in a "different camp" who are still, in reality, part of the "gospel camp."

This brings up another interesting observation. While it is a good idea to consult commentaries on the four Gospels that are written by both Calvinists and Arminians, the very nature of commentaries means that the differences between a commentary by an Arminian scholar and a Calvinistic scholar are not as pronounced as we might expect. This is due largely to the tendency of commentaries on the Gospels to focus on matters of history, culture, syntax, structure, and comparison with parallel accounts.

Nevertheless, if I am preaching from Matthew's Gospel, I will want to consult both D. A. Carson's comments in the Expositor's Bible Commentary series for a more Calvinistic perspective and Grant Osborne's volume on Matthew in the Exegetical Commentary on the New Testament series for a more Arminian take on matters.

For a commentary on Mark's Gospel from an Arminian, turn to *The Gospel of Mark: A Socio-Rhetorical Commentary* by Ben Witherington III. For a more Calvinistic counterpart, try James R. Edwards's volume in the Pillar New Testament Commentary series.

When preaching from the Gospel of Luke, I will consult Joel Green's volume in the New International Commentary on the New Testament series for a more Arminian view, as well as

Darrell Bock's volumes in the Baker Exegetical Commentary on the New Testament for a more Calvinistic slant.

Finally, the Gospel of John is served well by two leading commentaries from both theological perspectives. Once again, D. A. Carson writes from a Calvinistic perspective in his volume in the Pillar New Testament Commentary, while Craig S. Keener, a scholar from a more Arminian persuasion, has written a two-volume work titled *The Gospel of John: A Commentary.*

3. Admit tension and mystery rather than falling prey to reductionism. This theme has been prominent throughout this chapter. Yet I cannot emphasize it enough for those who take the Gospels seriously and wish to preserve the Evangelists' unique emphases—as well as the unique emphases of Jesus. D. A. Carson addressed the tension of divine sovereignty and human responsibility some thirty-five years ago in his Ph.D. dissertation at Cambridge University. He wrestled particularly with this tension in the Gospel of John, and his conclusion is well worth pondering by both Calvinists and Arminians. He writes: "There is no escape from the sovereignty-responsibility tension, except by moving so far from the biblical data that either the picture of God or the picture of man bears little resemblance to their portraits as assembled from the scriptural texts themselves."[15] Those who think they can resolve all the tension are simply deluded, Carson claims. "Rather, if you wish to convince me that your theology in this matter is more essentially Christian than my own, you must show me how your shaping of the tension better conforms to the biblical data than mine does."[16]

4. Point out common ground. While we must not deny or downplay the differences between Calvinists and Arminians, we must be careful to show the common ground shared by both systems. Pastors and theologians in both groups are deeply committed to the gospel. Both Arminians and Calvinists take the warning against apostasy in Matthew 24:4–14 seriously, affirming that those who do not stand firm to the end will not be saved. Arminians will tend to argue that this group includes genuine "possessors" who have been redeemed but will lose their salvation because they do not endure. Calvinists will tend to argue that those who apostatize show themselves to be "professors"— those who profess allegiance to Christ but whose salvation was never real in the first place. Although this difference is significant, it does not change the urgency of the warning. Both Calvinists and Arminians argue that perseverance is a necessary aspect of the salvation of God's people.

A Final Thought

I am not a prophet nor the son of a prophet, but I think I can accurately predict that the divide between Calvinists and Arminians will remain until Christ returns. Until then, may our preaching of the gospel texts that expose this divide lead people to wonder and worship rather than to anger and despair. May we preach the text rather than our theological system, acknowledging that while our theological system shapes the way we understand the text, our theological system ultimately derives from the text. May we preach the special standing we have before God based on his choice of us as well as the need to persevere and remain in his Son, Jesus Christ. May our preaching of the words and works of Jesus cause our listeners to rise up and identify more with Jesus Christ than with John Calvin or Jacob Arminius.

7

PREACHING WHAT JESUS SAYS ABOUT THE LAW OF MOSES

During the French Revolution of the late 1700s, revolutionary leader Maximilien de Robespierre and his confederates were adamant about establishing a new order by tearing down the old.[1] They completely changed the calendar, renaming years, months, and days of the week. They lengthened the seven-day week to a ten-day week. They gave new names to the streets and boulevards of Paris. They attempted to destroy France's past to establish something new. But the revolution was short-lived, and Robespierre was executed in July 1794.

When Jesus began preaching that the kingdom of God had arrived and that a new order had come, his listeners wondered what he intended to do with the old. They wanted to know where Jesus stood in relationship to the law of Moses. Did he affirm its ongoing validity? Did he intend to replace it? These are still pressing questions for listeners today. Exactly what did Jesus say about the law of Moses? How should Jesus' followers relate to it? This chapter will explore how each of the four Gospels presents what Jesus says about the law of Moses. In the process, I will suggest some ways we can help our listeners understand these bold, sometimes enigmatic sayings.

The Gospel of Matthew

The most definitive statement made by Jesus about his relationship to the law of Moses resides in Matthew. The occasion for this statement was Jesus' Sermon on the Mount, and the statement appears in Matthew 5:17–20. Obviously, those preaching a sermon series on Matthew or on the Sermon on the Mount will have occasion to preach it. Those who are preaching in one of the other Gospels will certainly want to look at it as a north star whenever they run into the question of how Jesus wants his followers to view the law of Moses. You may even want to insert a sermon on this text into a series on one of the other three Gospels.

Before looking at the text itself, it is helpful to remind ourselves and our listeners how the Hebrew Bible, or Old Testament, itself views the Law. In my experience, I have found that pastors and the churches they serve often begin with what Paul says about the law of Moses and use that as a grid for understanding the role of the Law in ancient Israel. But this leads us to assume that the original or only role of the Law was to expose people's sinfulness. No wonder contemporary believers often treat the Law "like a white elephant gift from a relative. It can hardly be thrown out, yet no one wants it in a prominent place."[2]

A careful reading of Exodus and Deuteronomy reveals that the law of Moses was a gracious gift of Yahweh given to a redeemed community. The historical prologue affirms this: "I am the Lord your God, who brought you out of Egypt, out of the land of slavery" (Exod. 20:2; Deut. 5:6). God had already saved, already redeemed the people of Israel *before* they received the law of Moses.

106

Furthermore, the words they received were words of life (Deut. 32:47). When Moses delivered these words to God's people, he told them to keep these words "so that you may live and prosper and prolong your days in the land that you will possess" (Deut. 5:32–33; see also 30:19). Also, according to Deuteronomy 4:8, possessing the Law was a sign of greatness, not of disadvantage (see also Exod. 19:5–6). Listeners who think that having such a long list of regulations—613 as counted by the Jewish rabbis—was a burden forget that these laws, many of them case laws, helped God's people figure out how to apply the Ten Commandments in sticky situations.[3] Americans who live in the United States are actually subject to thousands of local, state, and federal laws. Yet most of us do not feel the weight or burden of these laws as we go about our daily routines. We celebrate our freedom and recognize that there are laws in place to protect it. That's the tone of the books of Torah and other parts of the Old Testament, notably Psalm 119. There was simply no hint in Exodus or Deuteronomy or anywhere else in the Old Testament that the Law was a burden or that people could be justified by keeping the Law.

However, during the intertestamental period, the Pharisees proposed a solution to the problem of disobedience that had long plagued the nation of Israel and had led them into captivity. Their solution was to "build a fence around the Law" to help people obey it.[4] This fence consisted of piling on additional laws that were designed to help God's people keep the laws in the Mosaic code. By the time Jesus began his ministry, this system had become a burden and, in fact, a substitute for pure and undefiled religion.

It is in this context that Jesus proclaimed his Sermon on the Mount and offered these words on his relationship to the law of Moses:

Do not think that I have come to abolish the Law or the Prophets; I have not come to abolish them but to fulfill them. For truly I tell you, until heaven and earth disappear, not the smallest letter, not the least stroke of a pen, will by any means disappear from the Law until everything is accomplished. Therefore anyone who sets aside one of the least of these commands and teaches others accordingly will be called least in the kingdom of heaven, but whoever practices and teaches these commands will be called great in the kingdom of heaven. For I tell you that unless your righteousness surpasses that of the Pharisees and the teachers of the law, you will certainly not enter the kingdom of heaven. (Matt. 5:17–20)

There are four key points we need to make to our listeners—and first to ourselves—to help us navigate the question of how the Law relates to Jesus and his followers.

1. Jesus did not come to abolish the Law. Even though Jesus brought a new order, his plan did not include doing away with the Law. He did not come on a crusade to replace the Law or, by extension, the entire Hebrew Bible. I like to point my listeners back to Matthew 4:1–11 to show them that Jesus used the law of Moses to resist temptation. When tempted by Satan, Jesus quoted portions of Deuteronomy and the Psalms as his basis for what he was going to do and not going to do. This is an important point to make since too many believers over the years have treated the next statement about Jesus fulfilling the Law as a statement about abolishing it. As we will see, this is clearly not the case.

2. Jesus came to fulfill the Law. The term *fulfill* is extremely important to define. Some would like to translate it "confirm" or "establish," emphasizing that Jesus' ministry validates the ongoing authority of the Mosaic law for Jesus' followers. Theonomists, or reconstructionists, gave some momentum to this view a few years ago.[5] At the other end of the spectrum, others suggest, as noted above, that "fulfill" means Jesus has brought the Law to an end. He is finished with the Law, and it is simply time to move on. However, the emphasis is on bringing the law of Moses to its full, complete, intended expression. D. A. Carson comments: "Jesus fulfills the Law and the Prophets in that they point to him, and he is their fulfillment."[6] Likewise, Vern Poythress writes: "What the law foreshadowed and embodied in symbols and shadows is now coming into realization. What was earthly and preliminary in the function of the law is now fulfilled in heavenly realities. Jesus' teaching represents not simply the reiteration of the law but a step forward, bringing the purposes of the law into realization."[7] Jesus and his teaching, then, is the reality to which the law of Moses pointed.

To reinforce his point, Jesus makes a most striking statement about the authority, as well as the accuracy, of the Law and the Prophets. He asserts that Scripture's authority extends even to its smallest letter and to its smallest pen stroke. It may help your listeners appreciate what Jesus says if you visualize it for them. The "smallest letter"— or "jot" in some translations— was the Hebrew letter *yod*. When preaching this text, I usually instruct listeners to turn back to Psalm 119:73, the beginning of eight verses that all begin with the Hebrew letter *yod*. Many editions of the English Bible print the actual Hebrew letter above Psalm 119:73. The "smallest stroke" or "tittle" is simply a tiny brush stroke. Again, I point listeners to the Hebrew letter before Psalm 119:25, the *daleth*. If they compare this with the Hebrew letter *resh* which stands before Psalm 119:153, they can see how a small brush stroke closes the gap, distinguishing a *daleth* from a *resh*. Jesus' illustration is designed to say: "I have no plans to do away with the Law and the Prophets. They have lasting, abiding significance."

3. Jesus expects his followers to practice and teach the commands in the Law and Prophets. The word *therefore* at the beginning of Matthew 5:19 signals that Jesus is drawing a conclusion. His conclusion is that his followers must not set aside what the Law and Prophets command but rather practice and teach them. This, of course, raises a huge question. Are the commandments to be practiced and taught in the same way they were practiced and taught before Jesus came? R. T. France provides a careful answer, and his answer is worth pondering:

> The use of the verb "do" in v. 19 is easily read as meaning that the rules of the OT law must still be followed as they were before Jesus came, and thus as reinforcing the "righteousness of the scribes and Pharisees" which the next verse will disparage. But if that is what Matthew intended these words to mean, he would here be contradicting the whole tenor of the NT by declaring that, for instance, the sacrificial and food laws of the OT are still binding on Jesus' disciples—and surely by the time Matthew wrote Christians were already broadly agreed that they were no longer required. In light of the emphasis on fulfillment that has introduced this passage and which will be central to what follows we can only suppose therefore that he had in mind a different kind of "doing" from that of the scribes and Pharisees, a "doing" appropriate to the time of fulfillment. That will mean in effect the keeping of the law as it is now interpreted by Jesus

himself, and it will be the role of vv. 20–48 to explain what this means in practice.[8]

How, then, can we do this? Craig Blomberg answers: "Every Old Testament commandment must today be filtered through a grid of fulfillment in Christ to see how its application may have changed."[9] He continues:

We must avoid two often-held extremes that the text does not justify. One argues that all Old Testament teaching not rescinded in the New Testament is still in force. The other argues that all Old Testament teaching not reaffirmed in the New Testament is no longer in force. 2 Tim. 3:16 requires us to argue that *every* Old Testament law is somehow still relevant for Christians. But *none* of it can be applied until we understand how it has been fulfilled in Christ.[10]

4. Jesus expects a greater righteousness than mere law keeping. When I unpack Matthew 5:20 for my listeners, I will tell them that what Jesus says here strikes me as ridiculous! How can anyone out-do the Pharisees when it comes to righteousness? That resembles saying that unless you can sing better than Faith Hill or Josh Groban, you cannot sing in church. Or it is like saying that unless you can play basketball better than LeBron James, you should not bother trying out for your high school team! Yet there was a fatal flaw in the righteousness of the Pharisees. They created a system of righteousness that gave people a false sense of security. I remember the old rule I had to follow when I was a boy and wanted to go swimming. The rule was that I could not swim an hour after eating. Supposedly, this would prevent me from sinking to the bottom of the pool if I cramped up because of the food I had eaten. Today we know better. Eating a meal before jumping into a pool does not cause cramping! The rule may have sounded impressive, but like the traditions of the Pharisees, it did not really accomplish anything.

R. T. France insightfully explains what Jesus has done in Matthew 5:17–20. There is "on the one hand a tendency to claim in line with Paul's 'freedom from the law' teaching, that the OT laws no longer matter and can be abandoned."[11] Jesus deals with that tendency in verses 17–19. There is "on the other hand a tendency to emulate the scribes and the Pharisees in careful literal observance of the law as if nothing had changed with the coming of the Messiah."[12] Jesus deals with this tendency in verse 20, and then he illustrates it with the examples that follow in verses 21–47. In these six examples in Matthew 5:21–47, Jesus shows the kind of righteousness to which the law of Moses pointed. Ironically, the righteousness of the Pharisees actually bypassed rather than protected true obedience to God's laws. In another significant conversation (Matt. 22:34–40), Jesus cuts to the heart of what the Law really requires. We will consider this below.

The Gospel of Mark

When we turn to Mark, it almost seems like Jesus is not interested in the Law. Thomas Schreiner has observed, "The law plays a more important role in both Matthew and Luke than in Mark."[13] Mark does not record what Jesus says about the Law in his Sermon on the Mount as does Matthew 5:17–20. Nor does Mark record what Luke 24:13–49 does when it records Jesus' explanation to his disciples about how the Scriptures, including the Law, pointed forward to himself.

However, like Matthew and Luke, Mark's Gospel records some of Jesus' encounters with the Pharisees, and in these encounters what Jesus says gives us a window into how he viewed himself in relationship to the Law. When Jesus was questioned as to why his disciples did not fast (see Mark 2:18–22), he brought up the image of a wedding feast, likely alluding to the feast of the Messiah prophesied in Isaiah 25:6. His point was that "the fulfillment of God's promises does not call for fasting but feasting."[14] Jesus then shifts to the images of sewing a patch of unshrunk cloth on an old garment or pouring new wine into old wineskins. These practices simply do not work! The point is that a new order has arrived. "Jesus does not merely represent a restoration or patching up of the Torah, but his coming means that the Torah must be interpreted in light of him."[15] The very next accounts deal with alleged violations of the Sabbath by Jesus and his disciples (Mark 2:23–3:6). But his responses make clear that he, the Son of Man, takes precedence over the Sabbath. The Son of Man is Lord of the Sabbath, not the other way around.

Especially significant is Jesus' healing of the woman who had a hemorrhage of blood for twelve years and his raising of a twelve-year-old girl from death (Mark 5:24–43). His words to them betray no concern for uncleanness. After all, the law of Moses taught that a woman who had a discharge of blood was unclean, and anyone who touched her was unclean as well (see Lev. 15:25–27). Likewise, the Law clearly taught that any-one who touched the dead was unclean (see Lev. 21:1, 11; 22:4; Num. 5:2). However, as Schreiner notes, the old rules do not apply to Jesus![16] When the unclean woman touched Jesus, she did not defile him. Rather, his power overwhelmed and healed her condition. When Jesus touched the twelve-year-old girl, he did not contract uncleanness. Rather, he brought her back to life. Schreiner comments: "These accounts suggest that the law is no longer central with the coming of the Christ. . . . The new age has arrived in his ministry."[17]

Another key discussion about the Law takes place in Mark 7:1–23 where Jesus castigates the Pharisees for their hypocrisy. Jesus does not criticize the law of Moses but accuses the Pharisees of "setting aside the commands of God in order to observe your own traditions!" (v. 9). Then Jesus tells the crowd where true defilement happens—in the human heart. He argues that "nothing that enters a person from the outside can defile them" (v. 18). In other words, what people eat does not make them unclean. Here Mark adds a crucial editorial remark. He writes: "In saying this, Jesus declared all foods clean" (v. 19). This is astounding! Jesus has moved beyond his critique of the traditions of the Pharisees to declare that the food laws in the law of Moses have been superseded.[18] Here is an example of discontinuity between life under the Mosaic covenant and life under the new covenant. Eating rabbit stew, pork chops, or prawns would now be acceptable! The list of unclean animals in Leviticus 11:1–23 and Deuteronomy 14:3–20 no longer applies. Jesus has the authority not only to set aside the traditions of the elders but even a particular set of instructions in the law of Moses itself!

We should also note that Mark includes Jesus' answer to the controversial question about what is the most important commandment of all the commandments in the Law (Mark 12:28–34; Matt. 22:34–40). It is no surprise that one of the teachers of the law would raise this question. After all, these professional scribes and scholars devoted their lives to studying, classifying, and categorizing the laws in the Torah. Jesus' answer comes without any qualification or reservation. He identifies the command to "love God" in Deuteronomy 6:4–5 as most important and the command to "love your neighbor as yourself" in Leviticus 19:18 as the second.

Timothy Keller, pastor of Redeemer Presbyterian Church in Manhattan, models a helpful way for preachers to explain the significance of Jesus' answer to their listeners:

> Here Jesus is going to the very heart of the core dilemma of ethics. Human thinkers have for centuries felt there was a tension between "Law" and "Love." Do I do the legal thing, or the loving thing? Jesus is not so much picking one or two rules over the others, nor is he choosing law over love, but rather he is showing that love is what fulfills the law. The law is not being fulfilled unless it is obeyed as a way of giving and showing love to God and others.[19]

While the Gospel of Mark does not record some of Jesus' more explicit pronouncements about the Law, there is a strong undercurrent of Jesus' authority over the Law. He is the central figure of the "new exodus" that Mark's Gospel announces.[20] Clearly, the law of Moses is not central in his kingdom. The core of the Law is, however. Life in the kingdom inaugurated by Jesus is all about loving God and loving neighbor.

The Gospel of Luke

Like the first two Synoptics, Luke's record of what Jesus says regarding the law of Moses reflects both continuity and discontinuity between the era of Mosaic law and the new era inaugurated by Christ. We must keep this balance before our listeners. When I preach on gospel texts in which Jesus addresses the law of Moses—whether aspects or the whole of it—I like to say: "Some things continue, some things do not continue." In Luke's Gospel, the Mosaic law's emphasis on caring for the needs of the marginalized certainly continues.[21] Yet Luke is the sole Evangelist to record Jesus' statement about inaugurating the new covenant when he shared his final Passover meal with his disciples (22:20).

When we preach from Luke and run into sayings of Jesus that raise questions about how he viewed the relationship he and his followers had with the Law, we do well to point to the resolution of Luke's Gospel as the definitive answer to this question. There are two aspects to consider.

The first, as previously noted, is Jesus' statement at the end of the final Passover meal he shared with his disciples. Luke 22:20 reports: "In the same way, after the supper he took the cup, saying, 'This cup is the new covenant in my blood, which is poured out for you.'" His death, then, was putting in force a new covenant. The terms of this new covenant, as spelled out in Jeremiah 31:31–33, Ezekiel 36:25–27, and Joel 2:28–32, did not anticipate the obliteration of the old covenant as much as an ability to carry out its terms. Both the apostle Paul (2 Cor. 3:6–18) and the writer of Hebrews (Heb. 8–9) will draw sharper contrasts between the old covenant and the new covenant. So we do well to communicate to our listeners, as Timothy Keller does, that "the coming of Christ changes Old Testament laws, yet they have some abiding validity."[22]

The second aspect to consider when we wrestle with how Luke portrays Jesus' view of the Law is how the Law, as well as the remainder of the Old Testament, points forward to Jesus. This emphasis dominates the final scenes of Luke's Gospel as Jesus converses with a couple of his disciples on the road to Emmaus and then with the Eleven in Jerusalem (24:13–49). His climactic statement is: "Everything must be fulfilled that is written about me in the Law of Moses, the Prophets, and the Psalms" (v. 44). Once again, the idea of "be fulfilled" is referring to more than the fulfillment of specific predictions. Bock observes: "Jesus is the topic of Scripture. . . . The events of his life are thus no surprise; they are in continuity with what God revealed throughout Scripture. It is fair to say that Jesus sees himself and his career outlined in the sacred texts of old. For Luke, Jesus is proclaimed through prophecy and pattern."[23] Certainly, the Gospel of Luke is moving from the law of Moses as the authority in the lives of God's people toward both the new covenant and the one who puts it into effect: Jesus the Messiah.

The Gospel of John

The key to understanding what Jesus says about the Law as recorded in the Gospel of John lies in the magnificent prologue in John 1:1–18. As Schreiner notes, "John does not focus on the law but on Christ, and this is evident from the high Christology of John's Gospel."[24] What John's prologue says about the Law reinforces the ideas of both continuity and discontinuity we have seen in the Synoptic Gospels. The definitive statement about the Law comes in John 1:17: "For the law was given through Moses; grace and truth came through Jesus Christ." Unfortunately some readers see only radical discontinuity here. Read on its own, John 1:17 appears to pit law versus grace. Yet the preceding sentence says: "Out of his fullness we have all received grace in place of grace already given." So the contrast is not between law and grace, but between the grace in the Mosaic law and the greater grace in Jesus Christ! In fact, "grace and truth" is an expression that has its origin in the law of Moses. It is the Greek expression of "love and faithfulness" found in Exodus 34:6. Certainly, we have a greater measure of grace in Christ than in the law. But grace replaces grace, not law.

This is an important emphasis, because Jesus presents himself in the first half of John's Gospel as the one who replaces some significant elements in the various institutions and festivals of Judaism.[25] Jesus is the new means of purification (2:1–12), the new temple (2:13–22), the new rabbi (John 3), and the new source of water (John 4). He is the one who supersedes and provides the blessings anticipated by the Sabbath (John 5), Passover (John 6), Feast of Tabernacles (John 7–9), and Dedication or Hanukkah (John 10).

Here is an example of how a preacher can handle the question of the Mosaic law in John. I have preached John 5 (the entire chapter) in three different contexts, titling the sermon "Too Religious for Your Own Good." The outline looks like this:

I. Jesus upsets the religious establishment by going against the religious traditions on which they relied to experience life with God (vv. 1–18).

    A. Jesus heals a man on the Sabbath in defiance of Jewish tradition (vv. 1–15).

    B. As a result, Jesus receives prosecution and persecution from the Jewish religious leaders who relied on their traditions to experience life with God (vv. 16–18).

        Transition—In the rest of John 5, Jesus offers a defense of his actions and identifies the source of the life that God offers.

II. The life you've always wanted comes from embracing Jesus rather than from religious traditions (vv. 19–47).

A. Jesus argues that he is the source of the life that God offers (vv. 21, 23b, 24–26, 39–40).

B. By contrast, their religious traditions failed to connect them to the life God offers.

    1. These traditions either hid or choked off God's love in their hearts (v. 42).

    2. These traditions impressed other people, but not God (v. 44).

C. Today, our religious traditions can take on a life of their own and keep us from experiencing God's love.

D. The challenge is to embrace Jesus and not reduce our relationship with him to religious traditions.

I developed both points inductively. The second one functioned as the sermon's big idea. In the first point, or movement, of the sermon, I explained how the religious leaders had developed a series of laws designed to keep people from breaking the Sabbath laws in the Mosaic code. Here, then, is a theme that is woven throughout the Gospels: Jesus' problem is not with the law of Moses but with how people tried to obey it. Their attempts to obey it actually betrayed a fundamental misunderstanding of where we locate the source of the life God wants us to have. This, of course, is the concern of the rest of the story. It is the Son who gives life, not adherence to the law of Moses or the traditions designed to protect it.

Subtle yet Direct

When Johann Sebastian Bach responded to the challenge of Frederick the Great to compose a six-part fugue—a musical piece in which a theme is repeated or imitated by successively entering voices, Bach's *Musical Offering* delivered to Frederick "as stark a rebuke of his beliefs and worldview as an absolute monarch has ever received."[26] Bach's scathing indictment was subtle, yet direct. His *Musical Offering* included ten canons—another compositional technique in which a melody is imitated more strictly than in a fugue. By including ten canons, Bach invoked the law of Moses, inferring that "there is a law higher than the king's law which is never changing."[27] One of the canons was inscribed, "As the notes ascend, so may the glory of the king." Yet the fifth canon is the musical equivalent of an optical illusion. While it rises to a higher key each time it is played, it ends up in the same key it started—only an octave higher. It appears that "Bach is commenting on the distinction between the apparent glory of the king and the fact of his humble human estate, bound to a world of flaws and sin just like the rest of us."[28]

At times this is what Jesus does when addressing the Law. He uses subtlety to make strong statements about how he supersedes the Law. His parable about the wineskins is a case in point (Mark 2:21–22). At other times he is much more direct, claiming to be the fulfillment of the Law (Matt. 5:17–20; Luke 24:44). In the end, the challenge of preaching what Jesus says about the law of Moses boils down to integrating his direct statements and his subtle statements. When we listen attentively to what Jesus says, we will hear him saying that the Law points forward to him. He is not destroying it. Rather, he is the one who brings the Law to its full expression. Sound preaching from the Gospels celebrates this reality and leads listeners to worship the one whose shadow is found in the law code recorded by Moses so long ago.

8

PREACHING WHAT JESUS SAYS ABOUT PRAYER, FAITH, AND MIRACLES

Thirty years ago, a popular song by Billy Joel captured the disillusionment of a generation of steelworkers in Pennsylvania's Lehigh Valley who watched Bethlehem Steel decline and eventually close. Joel's song, "Allentown," lamented that the steelworkers were waiting for the promises their teachers gave—promises that they would be successful if they worked hard and behaved themselves. But these promises went unfulfilled, and the steelworkers found themselves discouraged and stuck in Allentown, waiting for the life they had been promised but had never found.

I find a similar mood among many listeners when I preach on what Jesus says about prayer, faith, and even miracles. They tell me they have responded to Jesus' call to ask, but they have not received. They have sought but have not found the object of their search. They have knocked, but no door has been opened. They have exercised faith, but the mountains remain unmoved. They have watched loved ones waste away from disease while Jesus, the one who was "healing every disease and sickness among the people" (Matt. 4:23), seemed to do nothing.

How, then, do we preach on matters where Jesus seems to promise more than he actually delivers? What can we say to those who suspect that Jesus has changed his modus operandi—that he does not deliver on his promises today as he did in the first century when he walked on the earth? This chapter will explore how to preach what Jesus says about prayer, faith, and miracles.

When Prayer Gets You Stones, Snakes, and Scorpions

It is no secret that Jesus makes bold statements about prayer. In his Sermon on the Mount, he declares: "Ask and it will be given to you; seek and you will find; knock and the door will be opened to you. For everyone who asks receives; the one who seeks finds; and to the one who knocks, the door will be opened" (Matt. 7:7–8). Whenever I preach this text, or the parallel passage in Luke 11:9–10, I tell my listeners that Jesus was adamant about the point he was making. We know this because he says it once and then repeats it. There is no hesitation, no qualification on the part of Jesus. His three images—asking, seeking, and knocking—scream out that prayer works.

But does prayer really work like Jesus says it does? Jesus obviously anticipates this objection because he deals with it in his very next statement: "Which of you, if your son asks for bread, will give him a stone? Or if he asks for a fish, will give him a snake? If you, then, though you are evil, know how to give good gifts to your children, how much more will your Father in heaven give good gifts to those who ask him!" (Matt. 7:9–11).

When I preach about how Jesus handled the unstated objection that prayer does not really work, I tell people that Jesus answers the objection by drawing a contrast between earthly fathers and our heavenly Father. Jesus begins with two examples related to earthly fathers. He presents both examples as questions, and both questions expect "no" answers.[1] No father will give his child a stone when the request is for bread. No father will give a child a snake in response to a request for a fish. The power of these images turns on how similar they appear from a distance. Before the uniform look of loaves of bread in plastic wrappers on a modern supermarket shelf, a round loaf of bread could easily be confused with a stone when viewed from a distance. Furthermore, the Sea of Galilee was known for a catfish that looked like an eel. From a distance, then, this fish could be confused with a snake. In Luke's account, he substitutes a scorpion for an egg in place of a snake for a fish (11:12). Once again, from a distance the body of a large, white scorpion could be mistaken for an egg. But no earthly father is going to give a stone in place of bread or a snake in place of an eel or a scorpion in place of an egg.

Jesus draws the contrast between earthly fathers and our heavenly Father with a "how much more" argument: "If you, then, though you are evil, know how to give good gifts to your children, how much more will your Father in heaven give good gifts to those who ask him!" (Matt. 7:11). The logic is not hard to follow. If earthly fathers who are sinful—and even the best of earthly fathers are sinful—give good gifts, how much more will our heavenly Father who is perfect give good gifts. In Luke's account, the gift is the Holy Spirit (11:13). There is no contradiction here, because for Luke the gift of God's Holy Spirit is the ultimate good gift—the One who provides God's presence, guidance, and intimacy.[2]

Here it is important for preachers to help listeners hear Jesus' words on prayer in his larger context. As D. A. Carson observes, Jesus' Sermon on the Mount has begun with an acknowledgment of personal bankruptcy (Matt. 5:3) and has already provided a model prayer (Matt. 6:9–13).[3] Matthew 7:7–11 follows with a call for persistence based on the assurance that this prayer will be heard. "But such praying is not for selfish ends but always for the glory of God according to kingdom concerns."[4] Indeed, the very gifts articulated in the Beatitudes (Matt. 5:3–12) as well as the requests made in the model prayer testify to the kingdom-focus of the requests. Bock puts it nicely in his comment on Luke 11:13: "The passage is not simply a blank-check request, but a blank-check request for the necessities of the spiritual life, such as those mentioned in the Lord's Prayer and those related to spiritual well-being."[5]

Laura Story's song "Blessings" grasps the import of Jesus' words. Her song grew out of her own struggle with unanswered prayer. When her husband, Martin Elvington, was diagnosed with a brain tumor, she asked: "Why didn't you just fix it, God? You're all powerful and all loving . . . just fix it."[6] Story's song recognizes that when we pray for blessings, peace, comfort, protection, healing, prosperity, and relief from suffering, God indeed hears our prayers. Yet he loves us too much to give us lesser things. Sometimes his "blessings come through raindrops." Sometimes his "healing comes through tears." It may even take "a thousand sleepless nights" to know that God is near. Story's song even wonders if what we perceive as troubles or trials are "God's mercies in disguise."

With God, there is no bait and switch. Preachers will do well to return to the images Jesus used and remind their listeners how prayer works. Sometimes when I ask God for my daily bread, he gives me what resembles a rock. Sometimes when I ask God for a nourishing fish, he gives me what appears to be a snake. At other times when I ask God for an egg, he gives me what looks like a scorpion. The lesson is that God's good gifts do not always look good from a distance. He does not always give me what I pray for, what I want, or what I think I need. He gives me a good gift that is good according to his plans and purposes and glory, not mine.

This perspective stands behind all the statements in John's Gospel where Jesus makes promises about prayer that seem absolute and unqualified. "You may ask me for anything in my name, and I will do it" (John 14:14). "Very truly I tell you, my Father will give you whatever you ask in my name" (John 16:23). But these statements are not as unqualified as they seem at first glance. The very first promise recorded in John by Jesus about his response to his disciples' requests contains an important qualifier: "And I will do whatever you ask in my name, so that the Father may be glorified in the Son" (John 14:13). The determining factor for how prayers are answered lies with the glory of God.

Faith and the Unmoved Mountains

When I was a boy, I learned a song in Sunday school that proclaimed, "Faith in God can move a mighty mountain." But like many others, I struggled with that concept. Can I really move mountains through faith in God? Jesus seems to claim this on two occasions when he discusses faith with his disciples.

In the first instance, Jesus has returned from his transfiguration experience to find his disciples unable to drive out a demon from a boy who suffered with seizures. When his disciples came to him privately and asked why they were unable to drive out the demon, he replied: "Because you have so little faith. Truly I tell you, if you have faith as small as a mustard seed, you can say to this mountain, 'Move from here to there,' and it will move. Nothing will be impossible for you" (Matt. 17:20).

The second instance takes place the day after Jesus' so-called triumphal entry into Jerusalem a week prior to his death. When he cursed a fruitless fig tree and his disciples saw it wither, they asked him how it could wither so quickly. Jesus replied, "Truly I tell you, if you have faith and do not doubt, not only can you do what was done to the fig tree, but also you can say to this mountain, 'Go, throw yourself into the sea,' and it will be done. If you believe, you will receive whatever you ask for in prayer" (Matt. 21:21–22).

What are we to make of these claims? A close friend of mine attended the funeral of a young man who had died of cancer. My friend reported to me that the preacher, a prominent scholar and author whose name you might recognize, scolded the funeral attenders for not having enough faith. If they would have had enough faith, the preacher argued, this young man would have been healed by the Lord. Does this align with what Jesus was saying about mountain-moving faith?

The first observation to make is that the quality, not the size, of a disciple's faith is what matters. Jesus' statement in Matthew 17:20 is striking for its tension between "little faith" and "faith as small as a mustard seed." The former is regrettable, while the latter is powerful enough to move mountains! Carson is surely right when he suggests that the word translated "little faith" (*oligopistia*) probably refers to the poverty of their faith rather than to its littleness.[7] The issue, then, is not the quantity of faith but its quality. Grant Osborne notes that the faith to which Jesus refers "does not simply mean certitude that God will grant the request but rather a total dependence on the God who watches over his children."[8]

A second observation is that the notion of removing mountains was proverbial for overcoming great difficulties. This image occurs frequently in Isaiah (see 40:4; 49:11; 54:10) and appears once in the apostle Paul's writings (1 Cor. 13:2). So there is no need to read this literally. As Craig Blomberg observes, "Neither God nor Christ ever rearranged the topography of the land by supernatural intervention. Nor is a miracle necessary to move literal mountains, merely earth-moving equipment."[9]

A third observation has to do with the unqualified language—"nothing will be impossible" (Matt. 17:20) and "you will receive whatever you ask for in prayer" (Matt. 21:22). There is a qualifier, and it is the context in which Jesus uttered these words. The promise simply applies to whatever Jesus has given his disciples authority to do, including the exorcism they were unable to perform.

Blomberg nicely captures the balance that preachers must convey when they proclaim the instructions of Jesus about mountain-moving faith. Though his comment regards Matthew 17:20, it applies as well to Matthew 21:21–22:

> Verse 20 nevertheless provides a precious promise we dare not ignore. Much is not accomplished for the kingdom because we simply do not believe God will adequately empower us or else because we undertake various activities in our own strength rather than God's. Yet we must recognize the limitations of this promise, in light of other Scriptures, and not use it to foist a guilt trip on ourselves or others when faith does not eliminate every calamity from our lives.[10]

There are always listeners who may question whether we are trying to soften Jesus' words or weasel our way out of his strong statements by qualifying them in ways he did not intend. After all, Jesus could have done more to qualify these statements. But he did not. It is worth reminding ourselves again that Jesus was an outstanding, fascinating teacher who was able to capture the attention of his audience without the use of modern-day audiovisual materials and props.[11] The reason Jesus did not qualify his words stems from the kind of techniques he used when he spoke. Robert Stein identifies the following: overstatement, hyperbole, pun, simile, metaphor, proverb, riddle, paradox, a fortiori argumentation (in which the conclusion follows even more strongly from a previously accepted fact, as in Matt. 7:9–11), irony, the use of questions, parabolic or figurative actions, and poetry.[12] Many of these techniques operated on a bit of a "shock factor," and excessive qualification—the kind we appreciate in Western culture—would have diminished the force of his words. He expected people to understand the subtle qualifications he included, and he anticipated their familiarity with both the force and the limits of these techniques.

Miracles

Preachers also face a passel of difficulties when they preach the words of Jesus that lead to miracles. In a sense, then, the issue is not so much with what Jesus says but with the result of what he says. When Jesus told a man with a shriveled hand, "Stretch out your hand," the man's hand was completely restored (Mark 3:5). When Jesus rebuked the wind and said to the waves, "Quiet! Be still!" the wind died down and the sea became calm (Mark 4:39). When Jesus took a dead twelve-year-old by the hand and told her to get up, she immediately stood up and began to walk around (Mark 5:35–42). These words and the miracles that followed require preachers to address some questions our listeners will raise. Two, in particular, need to be addressed. First, are

Jesus' miracles really credible? Second, what was the purpose of these miracles and their inclusion in the gospel accounts?

The Credibility Concern

Although a sermon cannot be reduced to an apologetics lecture, there are times when wise preachers will address the questions and doubts of their listeners. In fact, as Tim Keller has often argued, if we want nonbelievers to find their way into our worship services, we must speak as if nonbelievers are present. Those who have grown up hearing the gospel stories of Jesus generally do not flinch when they hear that Jesus healed the sick or raised the dead or walked on water. But unchurched people do. They often question the credibility of Jesus' miracles. While our job is to *proclaim* the gospel story, there are times when we must show that the story is credible—including the parts that recount Jesus' miracles. To review a point made earlier, this means dealing with Haddon Robinson's second "functional question"—the one that he refers to as "the C. S. Lewis question." Is it really true? Can I buy this? Preachers will do well to anticipate where their listeners will ask such a question. After all, listeners will not apply an idea or respond to an exhortation that makes no logical sense to them.

Thankfully, some leading New Testament scholars have done some fine apologetic work on the miracles of Jesus. One of the most accessible discussions is Craig Blomberg's chapter on "Miracles" in his classic work *The Historical Reliability of the Gospels*. I find especially helpful his grid of objections. Roughly, the objections people raise to Jesus' miracles can be grouped in three categories: scientific, philosophical, and historical.[13] What follows is the kind of statement I will make from time to time in a sermon on a gospel text that contains a miracle of Jesus. Obviously I do not include such an apologetic word in every such sermon, but often I will distill Blomberg's discussion into a statement like this:

> Now, some of you can't get past what we just read. The gospel text we're reading just claimed that Jesus walked on water! That's unbelievable, right? It lacks credibility, right? You certainly don't believe that, right? Actually, yes, I do believe what the gospel writer claims, and let me tell you why. There are three basic objections to Jesus' miracles, and there is a reasonable answer to each one of them.
>
> The first objection is *scientific*: "The discovery of the natural, physical laws by which the universe operates has proved them impossible."[14] Here's the short answer to this objection. While Christians believe in natural laws or regular patterns in nature, they deny that a miracle must be a *violation* of such laws. Science cannot claim that all events are natural—only those that are regular, repeatable, and/or predictable. Just as human behavior can change the physical world by their actions—for example, climate change—so God can change it as well.[15] Interestingly, there is a greater acceptance in contemporary culture of the "paranormal"—uncanny occurrences that defy explanation by natural causes.
>
> A second objection is *philosophical*. This objection stems from the eighteenth-century philosopher David Hume, who claimed that when an apparently miraculous event occurs, the weight of probability favors that the event can more likely be explained in a nonmiraculous, natural way than in a miraculous, supernatural way. For example, it makes

no sense to accept the claim that Jesus raised Lazarus from death when the sheer number of people who have died without being raised make the odds against it insurmountable. The answer to this objection is that it proves too much. "If historians applied it consistently to their examination of human testimony, they would rule out everything unique or unusual that ever occurred, including things held to be non-miraculous."[16] For example, applying this kind of philosophical reasoning to the life of someone like Napoleon Bonaparte would lead to the conclusion that most of what we read about Napoleon is untrue since it is so unique.

A third and more prevalent objection in contemporary culture is *historical*. This objection centers around the principle of analogy—the argument that a historian has no right to accept as historical fact an account of a past event that has no analogy in the present. For example, there is no reason to accept a story about Jesus' raising someone from the dead because contemporary experience teaches that people are not raised from the dead. However, the principle of analogy is too limiting. To cite a frequently used illustration, "How could a 'historian' from ancient days who had lived all his life in the tropics, and who had no knowledge of anyone who had travelled to more temperate climates, ever come to believe in the existence of ice?"[17]

A related line of reasoning looks at the similarities between the miracle stories in the Gospels and the miracle stories in the apocryphal gospels, which evangelicals reject. Is it inconsistent to accept the account that says Jesus successfully commanded the storm to stop (Mark 4:39) and then reject the account that says Jesus successfully called for a child to be withered when the child scattered a pool of water Jesus had gathered while playing (*Infancy Gospel of Thomas* 3:1–3)? However, the apocryphal gospels, which sprang up a century or more after the New Testament Gospels, differ drastically in their description of Jesus' miracles. "The apocrypha seem to reflect belief in a God who works miracles 'on demand,' thereby compelling people to believe in Christianity. They often tell of wonders worked for vengeful, trivial, or heretical reasons, in a fashion hard to reconcile with the spirit of the Gospels."[18]

There is much more to say, of course, but even the paragraphs above may be too much for listeners to handle without being overwhelmed. Preachers will have to determine how much to say at a given time. In a series on the Gospels or on some aspect of the life of Jesus, preachers may well be able to drip these insights into four or five or six sermons rather than presenting them in one fire-hose blast.

Another excellent resource for preachers who want to dig deeper is the mammoth two-volume work by Craig S. Keener: *Miracles: The Credibility of the New Testament Accounts*. In the conclusion to this book, Keener makes a simple yet profound point that preachers will do well to communicate to their listeners. Keener observes: "Miracle claims, especially regarding healings, are by Western standards surprisingly common . . . in regions of the world where such events are expected."[19] It is simply not true, then, that no one in the modern world believes in miracles. Keener goes on to argue that the "assumption that genuine miracles are impossible is a historically and culturally conditioned premise. This premise is not shared by all intelligent or critical thinkers, and notably not by many people in non-Western cultures. This assumption is an interpretive grid, not a demonstrated fact." Furthermore, "history does not support a linear evolution of all cultures toward this position."[20]

It goes without saying that such argumentation will not immediately convince all, let alone hardened skeptics. But the presence of a preacher who has given thought to these issues and can supply an intelligible response can be used by God's Spirit to convince a skeptical listener of the veracity of the gospel accounts. For listeners who want more, the sermon is probably not the best place for a more detailed apologetic defense of miracles. This will best take place in private conversation, in a class devoted to miracles, or in some kind of guided reading program using the books discussed in this chapter as a starting point. Preachers cannot be distracted from *proclaiming* the miracle stories in the Gospels. But they must, as part of that proclamation, provide a sketch of why these miracle stories are credible.

The Purpose of Jesus' Miracles

A key issue when preaching the miracle stories of Jesus is their purpose. How preachers view the purpose of Jesus' miracles will determine how they apply them to their listeners. This can get a bit complicated due to the differing views evangelicals hold regarding to what extent Christians can expect to duplicate what their Savior did. At one end of the spectrum, cessationists hold that while God still works miracles, what Paul called "the gift of miracles" is not given to believers today. At the other end of the spectrum, another group of Christians believe that the church should expect to see and perform the kind of miracles that Jesus did as a testimony to the truth and power of the gospel.

Regardless of one's perspective, there is one matter on which all can agree, and it is really the crux when it comes to drawing out the purpose for Jesus' miracles. What we must preach is that Jesus' miracles establish the presence of the kingdom of God (see Matt. 12:28) and reveal his glory, testifying to and verifying his identify as Israel's Messiah and as the Son of God (see John 2:11; 20:30–31). This is what the gospel writers intended when they wove the miracle stories into their accounts. Preachers cannot afford to get so hung up on the "problem" of miracles that they fail to proclaim that Jesus' miracles testify to his identify and his power. Our challenge is to preach them in such a way that our listeners respond as Jesus' first disciples did and ask, "Who is this? Even the wind and the waves obey him!" (Mark 4:41).

For example, in a recent sermon series on Luke, I chose to preach several miracle stories together in one sermon on Luke 8:22–56. This text includes the miracle of Jesus' calming the story (vv. 22–25), his healing of a demon-possessed man (vv. 26–39), his healing of a woman with a chronic condition, and his raising of a dead girl (vv. 40–56). My big idea was that Jesus is worth trusting because he is more powerful than the most powerful forces in the universe. I arrived at this idea by showing how each of the stories portrays Jesus' power.

1. Jesus is more powerful than the forces of nature (vv. 22–25).
2. Jesus is more powerful than evil spiritual forces (vv. 26–39).
3. Jesus is more powerful than illness (vv. 43–48).
4. Jesus is more powerful than death (vv. 40–42, 49–56).

Then I addressed the objection that I know many of my listeners were raising in their minds: even though he performed these mighty acts of power, a lot of Jesus' followers throughout the centuries have been tormented or overcome by these very forces that Jesus defeated. His followers still get hurt, displaced, even killed by tornadoes. His followers are still tormented by evil spiritual forces. His followers still get cancer, Lyme disease, arthritis, and deadly strains of the flu. Jesus' followers still die. So how can this passage be an encouragement to us?

To answer this objection, I took my listeners back to Luke 8:1: "Jesus traveled about from one town and village to another, proclaiming the good news of the kingdom of God." The answer is that even though we still suffer in a broken world, we can trust Jesus to make everything right when he fully establishes the kingdom of God. The good news of the kingdom of God is that the reign of God—when creation is restored, death is destroyed, evil is removed—has entered the world in advance to work in the hearts of people. This means that we are living in the "already but not yet" phase of the kingdom of God. Right now, we see Jesus' power in some dramatic ways. I have a friend whom God healed from chronic knee pain. There is no other explanation for an instantaneous relief from his pain three decades ago. Yet he has been struggling in recent months with rheumatoid arthritis, and God has not seen fit to heal him from this. It is part of the "already but not yet" phase of the kingdom. We see Jesus' power in some dramatic ways, but final resolution and restoration is still future. Still, it is real, and it is coming! The stories in Luke 8:22–56 assure us of this.

The people to whom we preach desperately want to experience miracles that put an end to their suffering. The promise we hold out is that whenever life in a broken world overpowers us, there is someone we can trust. His name is Jesus, and he is more powerful than whatever threatens to overpower us.

The Ultimate Miracle

Jesus spoke, though, about a far greater miracle. The Gospel of Mark records three occasions on which Jesus told his followers that he, the Son of Man, would be killed and after three days rise again (8:31; 9:31; 10:34). The resurrection of Jesus Christ is the ultimate miracle. It gives us reason to pray, to exercise faith, and to worship the Son of God whose identity and power was confirmed by his miracles.

Following Jesus requires both a theology of suffering and a theology of glory. It means both taking up one's cross daily (Luke 9:23) and being "clothed with power from on high" as a result of Jesus' resurrection (Luke 24:49). When we embrace both the cross and the glory, we will be in a far better position to understand what Jesus says about prayer, faith, and miracles. We can pray with confidence, exercise mountain-moving faith, and relish the significance of the miracles Jesus accomplished through his words while here on earth. We will expect prayers to be answered, faith to release God's power, and the miraculous work of Christ in people's lives. Yet our present experience in the "already but not yet" tension shapes the way that we experience God's power. As C. S. Lewis wisely observed toward the end of his essay *The Weight of Glory*, "Meanwhile the cross comes before the crown, and tomorrow is a Monday morning."[21]

9

PREACHING WHAT JESUS SAYS TO THE PHARISEES

A few years ago, I served on a citizen task force to help protect our community against pornography. My family and I lived in the capital city of one of the western states at the time. The people who opposed the efforts of our task force were strip club operators and porn shop owners. But there was another opponent that I never expected: the town librarians. Now, I love libraries. I have spent hours in the town library of every community in which I have lived. On my days off, I am likely to hole up in a library if I am not able to go fly-fishing or watch a baseball game. So I was taken aback when I realized that a group of people I respected—librarians in my community—opposed our task force.

Of course they had different motives than the strip club operators and porn shop owners. These librarians were not trying to get porn magazines into the hands of everyone who came into the library. Their concern was censorship. They were ready to fight anybody who advocated any form of censoring material. So while their motives were quite different, these librarians ended up on the same side as the strip club operators and the porn shop owners.

Something similar happened in Jesus' day. You would expect Jesus' opponents to be the tax collectors and sinners. Because they ignored God's Word, we expect Jesus to blast them with his strongest words of condemnation. Instead, Jesus reserves his harshest words for a group with whom he may have had the most in common: the Pharisees. Yes, Jesus' most heated confrontations took place with the religious establishment, not the irreligious folks. The Pharisees with whom Jesus got sideways were the people who desperately wanted to please and obey God.

Two Challenges

Preaching the accounts in which Jesus blasts the Pharisees presents some unique challenges for preachers. First, when most Christians hear the term *Pharisee,* they have a negative reaction. Fair or unfair, *Pharisee* has become a byword for *hypocrite.* I remember sitting in the office of a biblical studies professor at a theological institution where I received training and listening to him rail against the "modern-day Pharisees" on the faculty. I went to his office to get help on a research paper, but at that moment he was incensed over what he perceived to be the tepid reaction from fellow professors at a faculty meeting where he had just read portions of Matthew 23. He slammed down his Bible on his desktop and growled, "They just don't get it. They don't realize they are modern-day Pharisees." Whether my professor was right or wrong, I left his office praying I would never become pharisaic in my life and ministry.

Christafari, a Christian reggae band, sings a song titled "Modern Day Pharisee." The lyrics use language as scathing as Jesus used to criticize the modern-day version of the Pharisees Jesus faced. It includes expressions such as *parasites, plastic smiles, hypocrites,* and *concrete hearts* to excoriate these modern-day Pharisees.[1]

Both my professor and the band Christafari may have been spot-on in their assessments, and I do not criticize them for using the Pharisee image to make their point. Yet, over the years, this approach has created a particular caricature of the Pharisees as the "bad guys." As we preach texts from the Gospels where the Pharisees play a key role, we must ask ourselves if this caricature is the truth, or if the matter is more complex. The better we understand the Pharisees and the reasons why Jesus blasted them and did not blast them, the better we will apply to our situation today the texts in which the Pharisees appear.

There is a second challenge, though, for preachers who intend to proclaim the gospel texts in which the Pharisees appear. In light of Jesus' patience and mercy toward people, how should we understand his harshness toward the Pharisees? After all, Jesus called them hypocrites, blind fools, blind guides, whitewashed tombs, snakes, children of hell, and a brood of vipers. Try calling the people to whom you preach those names, and see how long they last—or you last! What do we make of this approach, given the current stress in both the culture and the church on civility and tolerance?

Who Were the Pharisees?

The place to begin our quest is first to understand the Pharisees. Who were they? Where did they originate? What motivated them to believe and act the way they did?

The material on the Pharisees is legion. Any good commentary or New Testament introduction or Bible dictionary will provide you more than enough. But perhaps the following sketch will cut to the heart of the matter and give you some leads as to how you can talk about the Pharisees when you preach texts involving them. Before reading the sketch, though, try taking the following ten-question true-or-false quiz. You may wish to borrow or adapt the quiz for use with your listeners the next time you preach on one of Jesus' encounters with the Pharisees.

1. The Pharisees were laymen, that is, nonprofessional Bible scholars.
2. Rabbinic Judaism emerged out of the Pharisaic movement more than out of any other group.
3. The Pharisees were staunchly anti-Roman, but they trusted in obedience and not violence as the means of ridding the land of this foreign oppressor.
4. The Pharisees had a passion for obeying God, and their approach to helping their fellow citizens obey God involved "building a fence around the Torah."
5. Jesus has more in common theologically with the Pharisees than with any other Jewish group.
6. Jesus criticized the Pharisees harshly, calling them mean names like "snakes" and "fools."
7. Jesus had some civil, productive conversations with Pharisees.
8. Some Pharisees showed concern for Jesus' well-being and safety.
9. The Pharisees were fairly popular and well-received in their culture.
10. At least one Pharisee took responsibility for the burial of Jesus.

All right, how well do you know the Pharisees? The correct answer to all ten questions is true. For the details, read the following sketch.

Of course wise preachers recognize that attempts to reconstruct the history of the Pharisees have run into debates and conflicting answers. For example, Jacob Neusner "believes Josephus in his *Antiquities* has grossly exaggerated the power of the Pharisees in the pre-70 period."[2] Still, Neusner considers the Pharisees more influential and more distinct from other groups than does E. P. Sanders.[3] However, there is fairly widespread agreement on a number of conclusions.

Their Origin

Many scholars see the Pharisees as spiritual descendants of the Hasidim, a group of pious Jewish fighters who attached themselves to Maccabean opposition to the Seleucid king Antiochus IV Epiphanes, beginning in 167 b.c.[4] Whether or not the Pharisees descended from the Hasidim, "the name 'Pharisee' first surfaces when the Hasmonean ruler John Hyrcanus 1 (135/4–104 BC) persecuted the Pharisees for resisting the Hasmonean rule."[5]

Joachim Jeremias commented nearly half a century ago: "The first appearance of the Pharisees, in the second century BC, shows them already as an organized group. The first mention of them is in the two books of Maccabees, and 1 Macc. 2.42 calls them 'a company of Assideans' . . . who were mighty men of Israel, even all such as were voluntarily devoted unto the Law' (cf. 1 Macc. 7:13; II Macc. 14.6)."[6]

The Jewish historian Josephus, whose lengthiest descriptions of the Pharisees occur in his *Jewish War* 2.162–164, 166 and *Antiquities of the Jews* 18.12–15, estimates the number of Pharisees during the reign of Herod the Great at about six thousand.[7]

Their Teaching

Craig Blomberg contends that the Pharisees, whose name probably means separatists, "were a generally popular and prominent group of laymen who sought to apply the Torah to every area of life. Their primary domain was the synagogue, and their foremost concern was to create 'a fence around the Torah.'"[8] The expression "fence around the Torah" can be traced back to the Mishnah. The tractate 'Abot begins:

> A. Moses received Torah at Sinai and handed it on to Joshua, Joshua to elders, and elders to prophets.
>
> B. And prophets handed it on to the men of the great assembly.
>
> C. They said three things:
>
> > (1) Be prudent in judgment.
> >
> > (2) Raise up many disciples.
> >
> > (3) Make a fence for the Torah.[9]

Oskar Skarsaune explains: "Making a fence around the law means giving supplementary rulings that hinder a man or woman from even coming close to breaking a scriptural command. These supplementary rulings have no direct biblical foundation, but are meant to prevent one from getting into a situation in which one might break a biblical command."[10]

Three additional details may be helpful in understanding what the Pharisees taught. First, Burge, Cohick, and Green observe that "what distinguished the Pharisees from the other groups in Judaism was their emphasis on religious practice as an *individual, personal decision*. . . . Individual adherence to the law was one firm way to express Jewish cultural and religious identity. This helps explain the Pharisees' focus on tithing, Sabbath observance, and food purity law."[11] Second, as Skarsaune explains, "The Pharisees sought to make every Israelite a priest and every meal a temple meal. Their aim was to extend the sanctity of the temple."[12] Third, the Pharisees "remained staunchly anti-Roman but usually opposed violence as a means of ridding the land of its foreign oppressor. Instead they sought to teach people to obey God's laws so that God himself would provide a savior in response to his people's obedience."[13]

Their Interactions with Jesus

Before exploring the more acerbic clashes between Jesus and the Pharisees, we should note that the two had some interactions that were civil and even favorable. Jesus' well-known discussion with Nicodemus is one example (John 3:1–15). In Luke 7:36, Jesus accepts an invitation to be the dinner guest of a Pharisee, and on another occasion some Pharisees showed concern for Jesus' well-being and safety by urging him to leave the place where they were and informing him that Herod wanted to kill him (Luke 13:31). At least one Pharisee took the initiative to provide for Jesus' burial. Nicodemus, the Pharisee "who had earlier visited Jesus at night," accompanied Joseph of Arimathea and helped place Jesus' corpse in Joseph's tomb (John 19:38–42; see also Matt. 27:60). Joseph of Arimathea may have been a Pharisee, too. We know he was at least a prominent member of the Council, that is, the Sanhedrin (Mark 15:42).

Their Connection to Rabbinic Judaism

A final issue to consider concerns the connection of the Pharisees to the rabbinic Judaism that flourished after the destruction of the temple in A.D. 70. This issue is important because it determines the extent to which we can read the Mishnah as a window into the thinking and teaching of the Pharisees. James VanderKam, a noted scholar in early Judaism, offers this assessment: "It is usually thought that, with some changes, the Pharisaic standpoint and approach survived the destruction of 70 CE in the form of rabbinic Judaism, and that the early rabbinic texts such as the Mishnah incorporate many Pharisaic teachings."[14] Similarly, while D. A. Carson warns that "there can be no simple equation of Pharisee and Mishnaic rabbi," he grants that the Pharisees would have embraced most if not all 'proto-rabbis.'"[15] Thus, while "the Mishnah (ca. A.D. 200) cannot be read back into A.D. 30 as if Judaism had not faced the growth of Christianity and the shattering destruction of the temple and cultus . . . it preserves more traditional material than is sometimes thought."[16]

Whenever we preach texts from the Gospels in which the Pharisees appear, we will do our listeners well to nuance our descriptions so that our listeners gain a balanced view—one that emphasizes the positive traits of the Pharisees as well as their negative ones. This tactic is not an attempt at political correctness or social politeness. Rather, it will heighten our dismay at the negative effect that Pharisaism, for all of its good intentions, had on the general populace. The fact is, the Pharisees and Jesus shared significant common ground. Both took the Scriptures seriously; both were skilled at using the Scriptures; both believed in the resurrection of the dead; both held to a Messianic hope.[17] By contrast, Jesus had less in common with the Sadducees, who denied immortality, resurrection, angels, and demons.[18] So Jesus had much more in common theologically with the Pharisees. But "it was their focus on external formalities" and their "rigid emphasis" on these formalities that put the Pharisees at odds with Jesus.[19]

Why Did Jesus Blast the Pharisees?

Now we must wrestle with Jesus' harsh words and confrontations with the Pharisees. It will help us to see his concern. Then we will be in a better position to help our listeners understand why his approach was appropriate and not inconsistent with his ethic of love and the tone of his Sermon on the Mount.

Jesus' Woes to the Pharisees

Jesus' most blistering condemnation of the Pharisees comes in the texts where he pronounces woes upon them. Matthew 23:13–32 records seven woes, while Luke 11:37–54 records six. Wise preachers will point out that a pronouncement of woe upon an individual or group should not be taken as an expression of outrage against someone for a personal offense. Jesus should not be viewed in the same light as a driver who mutters a curse on another motorist who cuts in front of him. Rather, Jesus is speaking in the tradition of the prophets "who frequently cried woe against Israel's sins."[20]

David Turner notes that these oracles, or heavy words, "blend anger, grief, and alarm about the excruciating consequences that will come upon Israel due to its sin. . . . The palpable pathos of woe oracles is due to the prophet's solidarities. The prophets must speak for God, but in announcing oracles of judgment, the prophets know that they are announcing the doom of their own people."[21] Thus the prophets express anger as they speak for God, yet they are grief-stricken because they must direct this anger toward their own people.

Matthew's record of the seven woes Jesus pronounced on the Pharisees comes after Jesus has excoriated the Pharisees for not practicing what they preach (23:3b), for placing a great burden on people without helping them handle it (v. 4), and for acting out of self-promotion and pride (vv. 5–7).[22] Jesus' disciples, by contrast, are to pursue humility rather than honor, understanding that true greatness is defined by being a servant and that humility is what leads to exaltation (vv. 8–12). With this as an "introduction," Matthew proceeds to record Jesus' seven woes (vv. 13–32).

Although some scholars see the structure of the woes into three pairs followed by a climactic concluding woe,[23] D. A. Carson sees a chiastic pattern that focuses on "the centrality of rightly understanding the Scriptures—a theme that is reflected in all the preceding controversies." Carson suggests the following pattern:

A: First woe (v. 13)—failing to recognize Jesus as the Messiah

> B: Second woe (v. 15)—superficially zealous, yet doing more harm than good

>> C: Third woe (vv. 16–22)—misguided use of the Scripture

>>> D: Fourth woe (vv. 23–23)—fundamental failure to discern the thrust of Scripture

>> C′: Fifth woe (vv. 25–26)—misguided use of the Scripture

> B′: Sixth woe (vv. 27–28)—superficially zealous, yet doing more harm than good

A′: Seventh woe (vv. 29–32)—heirs of those who failed to recognize the prophets[24]

Throughout these woe statements, Jesus has accused the Pharisees of being "hypocrites" (see vv. 13, 15, 23, 25, 27). R. T. France astutely observes that the essential nature of this hypocrisy "is not deliberate deception but rather self-deceit, in that they are accused of having missed the point of true religion especially by focusing on minutiae and externals instead of on the essentials of the sort of life God really desires."[25]

As if this is not devastating enough, Jesus proceeds to call the Pharisees "snakes" and a "brood of vipers" before raising a question that functions as a definitive statement: "How will you escape being condemned to hell?" (v. 33).

The Gospel of Luke records a similar yet distinct pronouncement of woes by Jesus upon the Pharisees in Luke 11:37–54. There are at least three reasons that indicate Luke has recorded a different teaching event than Matthew.[26] First, the two passages have different settings. In Matthew 23, Jesus is in public discourse in Jerusalem, while Luke 11 places Jesus at a meal while he is on his way to Jerusalem. Second, virtually none of the wording of the woes in Matthew 23 matches the wording of the woes in Luke 11. Third, the order of the woes in the two passages is quite different. The significance of this is that Jesus' harsh condemnation of the Pharisees was not an isolated event.

In Luke 11:37–52, the tone seems less bombastic than in Matthew 23:13–32. Luke does not record Jesus calling the Pharisees hypocrites, nor does he call them blind or describe them with epithets like snakes or brood of vipers. Perhaps this is due to the timing of the two settings. While Matthew's setting for Jesus' woes is in Jerusalem during the final week of Jesus' life, Luke's setting happens earlier in his so-called travel narrative (9:51–19:44) while Jesus is on his way to Jerusalem. Only when the controversy between Jesus and the religious leaders escalates does his rhetoric become more heated. We will revisit this observation when we draw some conclusions toward the end of this chapter.

But even if the tone is less bombastic in Luke's account, the accusations are just as daunting and anger producing. According to Luke 11:53, when Jesus went outside after pronouncing his woes, the Pharisees and teachers of the law began to oppose him fiercely. The following is a summary of what Jesus condemned in his woes upon the Pharisees and experts in the law. Since the scribes or experts in the law interpreted the law and aided the Pharisees in their study of tradition, we should see the two groups as distinct yet closely related.[27] So when Jesus condemned one, the condemnation applies to both. The experts in the law certainly understood it this way when they took Jesus' woes on the Pharisees as a personal insult (v. 45).

1. *The Pharisees missed out on justice and the love of God through their scrupulous attention to minute details* (v. 42). Jesus does not say that tithing does not matter, even though the Pharisees took an approach that resembles tithing pieces of popcorn or carrot sticks or M&M candies. He said they "should have practiced the latter without leaving the former undone."

2. *The Pharisees sought notoriety when they should have pursued humility* (v. 43). Like hundreds of leaders before and since them, the Pharisees gravitated toward pride, loving the most important synagogue seats and the respectful greetings they received in the marketplaces.

3. *The Pharisees defiled the people with whom they came in contact* (v. 44). No Pharisees, let alone any who followed them, would have thought of coming in contact with a grave lest they would become ceremonially unclean. For this reason, graves in ancient Israel were marked with white paint. Ironically the Pharisees had become just like the graves they abhorred and avoided. Instead

of being agents of God's cleansing, Jesus says the Pharisees had become agents of defilement. Perhaps we are to hear Jesus even accusing the Pharisees of leading people to death![28]

4. *The experts in the law placed a burden on the people, rather than leading them into freedom* (v. 46). Basically, the scribes made the burden of law keeping heavier, with the result that people were spiritually crushed by their inability to obey the detailed demands. A classic example of this was the list of thirty-nine acts of labor listed in the Mishnah—acts that seem to reflect the situation in the first century when Jesus had his confrontations with the Pharisees. The list in *Shabbat* 7:2 includes making two loops, weaving two threads, trapping a deer, slaughtering a deer, writing two letters, erasing two letters in order to write two letters, putting out a fire, and kindling a fire.[29] *Shabbat* 8:2 forbids taking out enough ink on the Sabbath to write two letters or taking out enough eye shadow to shadow one eye.[30]

5. *The experts in the law failed to submit to godly leadership and, in fact, murdered God's prophets* (vv. 47–51). Jesus makes a rather sweeping accusation here, blaming the experts in the law for approving what their ancestors did in murdering the prophets. Therefore, they will be held responsible for the blood of all the prophets that was shed from the beginning to the end of Israel's history as written in the Hebrew Scriptures. The account of Abel's death, of course, appears in Genesis, the first book of the Hebrew Bible. Zechariah's death report occurs in 2 Chronicles (24:20–21), which is the last book in the Hebrew Bible.

6. *The experts in the law had missed out on knowing God and hindered others from knowing God as well* (v. 52). This is the most grievous charge of all! It is the ultimate tragedy since there is

nothing more valuable than knowing God (see Jer. 9:23–24). Not only had the experts of the law failed to know God; they had kept others from entering into God's kingdom. How ironic, considering that they viewed themselves as the instructors and protectors of truth!

Keeping Jesus' Harsh Words in Perspective

So what are we to make of such harsh, vitriolic language? If I heard other preachers in my denomination or my circle of friends using such stinging rhetoric, I would likely tell them to tone it down. This is especially true since I serve on the borders of a large Jewish community. I am especially sensitive to any language that reeks of anti-Semitism. How are we to respond to the way Jesus talked to those religious leaders with whom he shared some significant common ground? Preachers will do well to share the following five observations with their listeners. These observations are not intended to soften, minimize, or dilute Jesus' harsh words, let alone apologize for them. Rather, these observations offer a few perspectives to legitimize the strong, in-your-face language Jesus used.

First, Jesus was a Jew speaking to fellow Jewish people. This observation is obvious, but it is worth remembering in an age when people are sensitive—and sometimes overly sensitive—to anything that offends the sensibilities of others.

Second, Jesus was speaking in the tradition of the Old Testament prophets who thundered against Israel when warning of her sin. The expression "brood of vipers" was used by John the Baptist (Matt. 3:7). The year King Ahaz died, Isaiah told the Philistines not to rejoice that "the rod that struck you is broken" since "from the root of that snake [Ahaz!] will spring up a viper" (Isa. 14:29). The snake imagery even goes back as far as Moses.

In Deuteronomy 32:33, he says that the wine of the enemies of God "is the venom of serpents, the deadly poison of cobras."[31]

Third, a similar but broader observation is that "ancient rhetoric tended to be more colorful than most modern standards allow" and that Jesus' "diatribe" in Matthew 23 "should be read in that context."[32]

Fourth, as noted above, the bombastic language of Matthew 23 in comparison to the less harsh tone in Luke 11 is appropriate for the level of rejection given to Jesus as Israel's Messiah. Carson offers this thoughtful assessment:

> The literary context of the chapter is extremely important. Not only does Matthew 23 climax a series of controversies with the Jewish religious authorities (21:23–22:46), but it immediately follows the christologically crucial confrontation of 22:41–46. The question "What do you think about Christ?" raised by Jesus (22:42), "was not simply a theological curiosity which could be thrashed out in the seminar room.". . . It stands at the heart of the gospel.[33]

Fifth, Jesus' harsh words to the Pharisees are not inconsistent with his ethic of love and the tone of his Sermon on the Mount. Carson argues that those who make such a claim miss two things. First, they overlook the fact that "the love Jesus demands of his followers is more radical and more discerning than modern liberal sentimentality usually allows." Second, "the Sermon on the Mount, not less than Matthew 23, also presents Jesus as eschatological Judge who pronounces solemn malediction on those he does not recognize and who fail to do his word (7:1–23)."[34]

Mark Galli argues, "Jesus provokes the Pharisees not because he is a trouble-maker but because he is a lover. Yes, of even the Pharisees. And he judges that at this point in his ministry, the clearest, cleanest way to tell them they have strayed far from the ways of God is to confront them publicly."[35]

Suggestions for Preaching on Jesus' Harsh Words to the Pharisees

So how do we take what we have learned and allow it to shape the sermons we preach on those texts where Jesus blasts the Pharisees? Let me offer four suggestions.

First, because many of our listeners are predisposed to regard the Pharisees as "the bad guys," we must highlight the positive traits of these sectarians to provide an accurate picture. As Craig Blomberg explains, "Pharisees were the upstanding 'conservative evangelical pastors' of their day, strongly convinced of the inerrancy of Scripture and its sufficiency for guidance in every area of life, if only it could be properly interpreted."[36] Again, the concern here is not to soften the portrait of the Pharisees to keep from offending the sensibilities of late-modern listeners. Rather, it is to provide an accurate picture that will heighten these listeners' awareness of how they are not unlike the Pharisees! If we reinforce the stereotypical picture of the Pharisees as "the bad guys," few of our listeners will be in a position to admit their own Pharisaic tendencies.

Second, as a complement to the first suggestion, we must not use an expression like *modern-day Pharisee* indiscriminately in reference to people whose convictions are stricter than ours. For example, if a particular believer decides to abstain completely from alcohol, follow an ambitious program of reading through the Bible in ninety days, sets strict rules for her children's use of the Internet, and decides not to have a television in her home, is it fair to label her as a Pharisee? The answer depends entirely on the attitude with which the person holds these convictions. If she holds up these practices in an attention-gaining way, or if she communicates her practices in a smug, condescending way, then the epithet *Pharisee* applies. If she touts these practices as a mark of spirituality and looks down on Christians who drink in moderation, follow a less ambitious Bible reading program, and so forth, then her behavior can be labeled Pharisaic. However, it is unfair to call someone a Pharisee who holds stricter standards graciously and does not turn them into a litmus test for spirituality. Not only do we wrongly malign people when we call them Pharisees for holding to tighter convictions than we do, but we strip the term *Pharisee* of its power. We will do well to describe someone as a modern-day Pharisee only when he exhibits the pride and reductionism and legalism of the group with which Jesus was often at odds.

Third, we must understand Jesus' tone in criticizing the Pharisees within the unique context of first-century Judaism. This is an important issue because it shapes both our view of Jesus and the extent to which we adopt his tone in our own critiques of modern-day Pharisaism. As noted earlier in this chapter, Jesus' tone certainly fit in with the cultural norms of Judaism—both the first-century Judaism of his day and Judaism in the centuries prior to his earthly ministry. His language was strong and bold, yet it fit within the prophetic tradition. Listeners need to understand this. At the same time, we dare not apologize for or dilute Jesus' scathing denunciations of the Pharisees. We will help the cause of Christ when we show our listeners what was—and what is—at stake in Jesus' conflict with the Pharisees.

As far as adopting an approach similar to Jesus', we must pursue a tone that fits within our culture. This tone must not soften the message, nor must it overshadow the message. Over the years, I have visited Petersburg, Illinois, and nearby New Salem, more than three dozen times. Abraham Lincoln moved to the little village of New Salem in 1831 when he was twenty-two and lived there for six years. During this time, a Methodist circuit-riding preacher, Peter Cartwright, frequently preached "fire and brimstone" messages and had a reputation as a man who could thrash anyone who dared insult him and had no qualms about speaking harshly about those who opposed him. Reports of his ministry suggest that dozens came to faith in Christ as a result of his preaching. Contrast this with the approach of Billy Graham who preached unashamedly about the realities of sin and eternal judgment yet did not ridicule people or use condemning epithets against them.

Comparing Graham and Cartwright is, perhaps, like comparing apples and oranges. Both were the product of different times, and Graham took advantage of technology—namely television—which was more than a century away when Cartwright was denouncing sinners in the Sangamon River valley of Illinois. The point I wish to make is that Graham did not compromise the gospel by not calling people "broods of vipers" or "children of hell." Had he used the approach of Cartwright, or Jesus, for that matter, he may have turned off some listeners simply because this kind of rhetoric did not have the place in North America in the 1960s and 1970s that it did in frontier Illinois in the 1830s or in first-century Palestine.

Finally, and perhaps most significant, contemporary gospel preachers will do well to follow Jesus in warning his followers of the leaven of the Pharisees—hypocrisy (see Luke 12:1). In a recent sermon on Luke 11:29–54, I argued that Jesus singled out the Pharisees because they created a religious system that looked good on the outside but never dealt with the inside. The human problem, of course, is an inside problem—an unclean heart. Jesus said: "Now then, you Pharisees clean the outside of the cup and dish, but inside you are full of greed and wickedness" (Luke 11:39). What our people need to understand is that outward ritual without inner rebirth never gets to the core of our sin problem. No wonder Jesus talks to the Pharisee, Nicodemus, about the new birth (John 3:3)! No wonder that Peter, one of Jesus' closest disciples, later writes: "Praise be to the God and Father of our Lord Jesus Christ! In his great mercy he has given us new birth into a living hope through the resurrection of Jesus Christ from the dead" (1 Pet. 1:3). This new birth leads to an inner transformational process that happens over the lifetime of a believer (see 2 Cor. 3:18; Phil. 1:6).

Although the texts in the Gospels where Jesus blasts the Pharisees appear to be negative, strident texts, I find in them a ray of light that keeps believers on the path to freedom and life. These texts can steer people away from an approach that reduces spiritual disciplines to mere rituals. Spiritual disciplines are activities that open up believers to the life-changing power of God's Spirit. But the Pharisee in me (yes, that is a helpful moniker!) takes these means and turns them into ends. Instead of basing my self-evaluation on the fruit of the Spirit (Gal. 5:22–23), I opt instead for an activity-based spirituality. Rather than evaluating my life based on the presence of love, joy, peace, patience, and other fruit of the Spirit, I grade myself based on the amount and intensity of my Bible reading, praying, giving, and so forth. To be sure, these disciplines are important. I have not opened up myself to the Spirit's power without them. But they are only means, not ends. Pharisaic religion goes a step further, taking these activities and intensifying them until they become burdensome.

Another way to frame this is to tell people that "flow-chart theology" does not work. Life is too complex for that. Oddly, folks who have been Christ-followers for many years can succumb to such an approach. Rather than obeying God through the freedom we have in the Spirit of Christ, we retreat to the haven of rules and regulations. Instead of wrestling with how to glorify God in a situation, we prefer a cadre of detailed demands to keep us on the right track. However, what helps God's people love others is not a set of ten or twenty rules but rather the overflow of a life that has meditated deeply on the love and grace that God has shown to us in Christ. The question, then, to pose to our listeners is not, how religious are you? Rather, we ask: "Have you trusted the gospel and reflected deeply on it? Is your life overflowing from your joy over the gospel—the good news that Jesus Christ died for your sins and was raised to life so that you might walk in newness of life?" Only the gospel of the kingdom, and not Pharisaic religion, can help you walk with God.

The Shabbat Elevator in Ashkelon

The very first hotel I stayed in when I visited Israel was in Ashkelon. When I checked in on a Thursday evening and proceeded to a bank of elevators, I chose the one that had no line. This was a wise choice, I thought. But a bellhop suggested to me that I might not want to take that particular elevator because my room was on the fifth floor and because the elevator that had no line was a Shabbat elevator. I soon discovered that Shabbat elevators are designed to keep practicing Jewish people from violating the Sabbath. These elevators stop at every floor so that their riders do not need to push the buttons that instruct the elevators to stop at particular floors. Pushing these buttons on the Sabbath constitutes a violation of the Sabbath since this act amounts to "lighting a fire." It's lighting a fire because the signal is sent electronically! Trace this custom back to its source, and you will end up sitting in a synagogue in first-century Israel listening to a Pharisee expound on how to keep God's law.

As my experience demonstrates, it is fairly easy to spot the legacy of the Pharisees in other cultures in other lands. But where do we get off center and gravitate toward a Pharisaic approach to religion? How do we know when we are coming dangerously close to living as modern-day Pharisees? How can we help the people to whom we preach pursue pure and undefiled religion rather than religion that reduces godliness to mere ritual? The gospel texts in which Jesus encounters the Pharisees provide a treasure trove for preachers who wrestle with these questions. Our challenge is to preach them well, exposing the Pharisaic approach to religion for the damages it does to pleasing God. When we preach these texts well, our people will not respond by bashing the Pharisees—except for listeners who are modern-day Pharisees!—but by examining their own hearts to see whether their inside is full of greed and wickedness masked by religious activities or whether they contain Spirit-produced streams of living water from which pure and undefiled religion flows.

CONCLUSION

A lot of tourists drive by David Ben Gurion's retirement home in the Negev desert of southern Israel without stopping. This is understandable; many tourists have traveled to Israel to visit the sites associated with the Bible's history and figures like Abraham, David, and Jesus. But on a visit to Israel in the summer of 2004, the group with which I traveled stopped at the Sde Boker kibbutz home of the main founder and first prime minister of Israel.

Two items in Ben Gurion's modest home particularly struck me. One was the copy of Hal Lindsey's bestseller *The Late Great Planet Earth* on a stack of books on a chair beside Ben Gurion's desk. No, he was not trying to decide whether to embrace Lindsey's views on Bible prophecy. He simply liked to keep abreast of popular attitudes toward the modern State of Israel. The second item in Ben Gurion's home that struck me was a portrait hanging on the living room wall—a portrait of Abraham Lincoln. To Ben Gurion, Lincoln was a hero—the epitome of a leader.

What made Lincoln such a powerful leader? His words. As one Lincoln scholar argues, his words were his sword.[1] What he said empowered his presidency. When Lincoln spoke his Gettysburg Address or his Second Inaugural Address, what he said shaped the attitudes and values and vision of a nation.

In the same way, Jesus' power owed much to what he said. From the outset of his ministry, "the people were amazed as his teaching" (Mark 1:22). Mark 1:27 reports: "The people were all so amazed that they asked each other, 'What is this? A new teaching—and with authority!'"

Yet Jesus' words also saddened, confused, and angered his listeners. The young ruler with significant wealth went away sad (Luke 18:23). Jesus' parents did not understand what he was saying to them when he told them why he had ditched them to be in the temple (Luke 2:48–50). Nor did his disciples understand some of his words about his death (Luke 9:45; 18:34). Others accused him of being demon possessed and raving mad. "Why listen to him?" they said (John 10:20). On one occasion, when they did not like what they heard, his opponents even picked up stones to stone him (John 10:31).

The truth is, what Jesus says is not always easy to understand, digest, or accept. A friend of mine once quipped that he felt like preaching a series of sermons on "Things I Wish Jesus Had Never Said." Philip Yancey confesses: "Long after I came to recognize the enduring truth of the Beatitudes, I still brooded over the uncompromising harshness of the rest of Jesus' sermon. Its absolutist quality left me gasping."[2] What about those who say they like Jesus but not the church? Imagine their horror when they hear what Jesus says about hell. As I noted in a previous volume, some try to sidestep this issue by casting doubt on whether Jesus really said what the four Evangelists attribute to him.[3] But for those who take Jesus' words seriously, help is needed.

I trust this volume has given you some leads and some direction when it comes to preaching the hard sayings of Jesus. The high school from which three of my four children graduated chose this as their motto: "Enter here to learn; go forth to serve." That's similar to the invitation of this book: "Enter here to learn; go forth to preach." In this book we've looked at the trees and at some of the bark on those trees, but let's take stock of the forest, the big picture. Here are two final pleas that grow out of the forest of hard sayings we have explored.

First, do not avoid the hard sayings of Jesus. Some of the richest treasures we bring to our listeners will be found in them. Besides, these hard sayings keep us on our toes, helping us skirt some of the platitudes that sometimes plague preachers. How can we pronounce, with hymnwriter Robert Loveless, that "every day with Jesus is sweeter than the day before" when Jesus says that all who wish to come after him must deny themselves and take up their cross and follow him? As Mark Galli quips, what Jesus was really saying was "God loves you and has a difficult plan for your life."[4] Honest, forthright, thoughtful expositions of the hard sayings of Jesus will confront our listeners with the Jesus they never knew. Like Jesus' preaching, such preaching will cause division. Some people will get angry and leave. But others will abandon everything for the sake of the call.

Second, if we have learned anything, it is that we must think contextually and culturally to understand what Jesus meant by what he said. So many hard sayings come into sharper focus when we consider the world of first-century Judaism and the customs of life in an age without smart phones and air travel. We still may not always like what we hear. We may prefer operating from the maxim "a gentle tongue can break a bone" (Prov. 25:15), while Jesus' modus operandi is to blast his listeners with stinging rebuke. But when we consider what Jesus said in the context of his culture, his sayings will at least be more intelligible. Then his words will be able to do their work; they will be able to comfort us in our affliction or afflict us in our comfort.

I am still not sold on red-letter editions of the Bible. I do not want to be guilty of elevating Jesus' words so that they become a canon within a canon. But how can I not savor them and obsess over them and proclaim them to the listeners I love? Jesus' words are the words of life! As Jesus himself said: "Very truly I tell you, whoever hears my word and believes him who sent me has eternal life and will not be judged but has crossed over from death to life" (John 5:24). Keep in mind that he said this to those who were trying to kill him because they did not like what they were hearing (see John 5:18). Yes, Jesus' words, his hard sayings included, are wonderful words of life.

May God strengthen the old generation of preachers and raise up a new generation of preachers who are committed to understanding Jesus' words truly and proclaiming them clearly. Go forth to preach!

THE AUTHOR

Steven D. Mathewson is senior pastor of the Evangelical Free Church of Libertyville, Illinois, and teaches preaching for the doctoral program at Denver Seminary, the master of divinity program at Trinity Evangelical Divinity School, and the undergraduates at Moody Bible Institute. He is author of *The Art of Preaching Old Testament Narrative*. He received his doctoral degree in preaching from Gordon-Conwell Theological Seminary under the mentorship of respected professor and author Haddon Robinson. He has been a pastor for more than twenty-five years and has preached sequentially through each of the four Gospels. He and his wife, Priscilla, have four grown children and two grandchildren. In his spare time, Steve enjoys fly-fishing, hiking, and watching his youngest son play college football.

NOTES

Chapter 1: Preaching What Jesus Says That Is Harsh and Shocking

1. Leland Ryken, *How to Read the Bible as Literature* (Grand Rapids: Zondervan, 1984), 100.

2. D. A. Carson, "Matthew," in *Matthew and Mark,* The Expositor's Bible Commentary, rev. ed., vol. 9 (Grand Rapids: Zondervan, 2010), 184.

3. Craig L. Blomberg, *Matthew,* The New American Commentary (Nashville: Broadman, 1992), 109.

4. Carson, "Matthew," 185.

5. Haddon W. Robinson, *The Christian Salt and Light Company: A Contemporary Study of the Sermon on the Mount* (Grand Rapids: Discovery House, 1988), 143.

6. Ibid.

7. Grant R. Osborne, *Matthew,* Exegetical Commentary on the New Testament (Grand Rapids: Zondervan, 2010), 197.

8. Craig S. Keener, *The Gospel of John: A Commentary* (Peabody, MA: Hendrickson, 2003), 1:687.

9. Ibid., 1:688.

10. Ryken, *How to Read the Bible,* 99.

11. See David L. Turner, *Matthew*, Baker Exegetical Commentary on the New Testament (Grand Rapids: Baker Academic, 2008), 233.

12. R. T. France, *The Gospel of Matthew*, The New International Commentary on the New Testament (Grand Rapids: Eerdmans, 2007), 594–95.

13. Ibid., 595, note 24. France cites the following biblical passages: Deut. 23:18; 1 Sam. 17:43; 2 Sam. 16:9; Ps. 22:16, 20; Prov. 26:11; Phil. 3:2.

14. Ibid., 590.

15. Ibid., 591.

16. Carson, "Matthew," 336.

17. Ibid.

18. Blomberg, *Matthew*, 203.

19. Osborne, *Matthew*, 476.

20. Carson, "Matthew," 336. Carson notes that his final phrase, "conscious disputing of the indisputable" comes from G. C. Berkouwer.

21. See Matt. 26:69–75; Mark 14:66–72; Luke 22:54–62; John 18:15–18, 25–27. Jesus' triple "commission" of Peter in John 21:15–18 assures us that Peter's triple denial does not disqualify him from following and serving Jesus.

22. See Acts 7:58–8:3; 9:1–31.

23. Blomberg, *Matthew*, 204.

24. Darrell L. Bock, *Luke 9:51–24:53*, Baker Exegetical Commentary on the New Testament (Grand Rapids: Baker Academic, 1996), 1141.

25. Ibid., 1141–42.

26. Blomberg, *Matthew*, 204.

27. C. E. B. Cranfield, *The Gospel according to St. Mark*, The Cambridge Greek Testament Commentary (London: Cambridge University Press, 1959), 142.

28. Blomberg, *Matthew*, 204.

29. Klyne R. Snodgrass, *Stories with Intent: A Comprehensive Guide to the Parables of Jesus* (Grand Rapids: Eerdmans, 2008), 157–58.

30. Ibid., 160.

31. Ibid., 161.

32. Carson, "Matthew," 356.

33. David Wenham, *The Parables of Jesus* (Downers Grove, IL: InterVarsity, 1989), 244.

34. Nancy Gibbs and Michael Duffy, *The Presidents Club: Inside the World's Most Exclusive Fraternity* (New York: Simon & Schuster, 2012), 415.

35. Ibid., 10.

Chapter 2: Preaching What Jesus Says about the Radical Demands of Discipleship

1. Dietrich Bonhoeffer, *The Cost of Discipleship*, rev. ed. (New York: Macmillan, 1963), 99.

2. Eric Metaxas, *Bonhoeffer: Pastor, Martyr, Prophet, Spy* (Nashville: Thomas Nelson, 2010), 531–32.

3. Bonhoeffer, *The Cost of Discipleship*, 45.

4. Grant R. Osborne, *Matthew*, Zondervan Exegetical Commentary on the New Testament (Grand Rapids: Zondervan, 2010), 404.

5. Darrell L. Bock, *Luke 9:51–24:53*, Baker Exegetical Commentary on the New Testament (Grand Rapids: Baker Academic, 1996), 1284.

6. Idid.

7. Ibid., 1285.

8. Craig L. Blomberg, *Matthew*, The New American Commentary (Nashville: Broadman, 1992), 146–47.

9. Osborne, *Matthew*, 305–6.

10. D. A. Carson, "Matthew," in *Matthew and Mark*, The Expositor's Bible Commentary, rev. ed., vol. 9 (Grand Rapids: Zondervan, 2010), 247.

11. See Kenneth Bailey, *Through Peasant Eyes: More Lucan Parables* (Grand Rapids: Eerdmans, 1980), 26–27.

12. See Craig Keener, *A Commentary on the Gospel of Matthew* (Grand Rapids: Eerdmans, 1999), 276.

13. David L. Turner, *Matthew*, Baker Exegetical Commentary on the New Testament (Grand Rapids: Baker Academic, 2008), 240.

14. David Platt, *Radical: Taking Back Your Faith from the American Dream* (Colorado Springs: Multnomah, 2010), 119–24.

15. Darrell L. Bock, *Luke 1:1–9:50*, Baker Exegetical Commentary on the New Testament (Grand Rapids: Baker Academic, 1994), 852.

16. Eugene H. Peterson, *Eat This Book: A Conversation in the Art of Spiritual Reading* (Grand Rapids: Eerdmans, 2006), 16.

17. The literal translation of these words is "let him take up *his* cross."

18. Bonhoeffer, *The Cost of Discipleship*, 45.

19. Ibid., 60.

Chapter 3: Preaching What Jesus Says about Sex and Marriage

1. John Piper, *This Momentary Marriage: A Parable of Permanence* (Wheaton, IL: Crossway, 2009), 24.

2. Haddon W. Robinson, *The Christian Salt and Light Company: A Contemporary Study of the Sermon on the Mount* (Grand Rapids: Discovery House, 1988), 143.

3. Francis Brown, S. R. Driver, and Charles A. Briggs, *A Hebrew and English Lexicon of the Old Testament* (Oxford: Oxford University Press, 1907), 179–80.

4. See Allen P. Ross, *Creation and Blessing: A Guide to the Study and Exposition of Genesis* (Grand Rapids: Baker, 1988), 126.

5. Bruce K. Waltke and Cathi J. Fredricks, *Genesis: A Commentary* (Grand Rapids: Zondervan, 2001), 90.

6. J. Carl Laney, *The Divorce Myth: A Biblical Examination of Divorce and Remarriage* (Minneapolis: Bethany House, 1981), 62–81.

7. Stanley A. Ellisen, *Divorce and Remarriage in the Church* (Grand Rapids: Zondervan, 1977), 51–52.

8. Craig L. Blomberg, "Marriage, Divorce, Remarriage, and Celibacy: An Exegesis of Matthew 19:3–12," *Trinity Journal* NS 11 (1990): 188–89.

9. See D. A. Carson, "Matthew" in *Matthew and Mark,* The Expositor's Bible Commentary, rev. ed., vol. 9 (Grand Rapids: Zondervan, 2010), 466. Carson notes that the school of Hillel in Palestinian Judaism "extended the meaning [of "something indecent" in Deuteronomy

24:1] beyond sin to all kinds of real or imagined offenses, including an improperly cooked meal. The Hillelite R. Akiba permitted divorce in the case of a roving eye for prettier women (*m. Git.* 9:10)." The reference Carson includes at the end of his comment is to Mishnah tractate *Gittin*. See Jacob Neusner, *The Mishnah: A New Translation* (New Haven, CT: Yale University Press, 1988), 487.

10. Grant R. Osborne, *Matthew*, Exegetical Commentary on the New Testament (Grand Rapids: Zondervan, 2010), 706.

11. Carson, "Matthew," 473.

12. Osborne, *Matthew*, 706.

13. Ibid., 707.

14. R. T. France, *The Gospel of Matthew*, The New International Commentary on the New Testament (Grand Rapids: Eerdmans, 2007), 724.

15. Ibid. A notable exception is Origen, who read this literally and castrated himself. France cites Eusebius, *Ecclesiastical History*, 6.8.1–3.

16. Osborne, *Matthew*, 707.

17. James B. De Young, *Homosexuality: Contemporary Claims Examined in Light of the Bible and Other Ancient Literature and Law* (Grand Rapids: Kregel, 2000), 288–89.

18. Ibid., 289.

19. Thomas E. Schmidt, *Straight and Narrow?: Compassion and Clarity in the Homosexuality Debate* (Downers Grove, IL: InterVarsity, 1995), 172–73.

Chapter 4: Preaching What Jesus Says about Hell and Judgment

1. Harry S. Stout, Nathan O. Haths, and Kyle P. Farley, eds., *The Works of Jonathan Edwards,* vol. 22, *Sermons and Discourses 1739–1742* (New Haven, CT: Yale University Press, 2003), 412. This excerpt appears about a third of the way through the "Application" section of the sermon. For other editions, see John E. Smith, Harry S. Stout, and Kenneth P. Minkema, *A Jonathan Edwards Reader* (New Haven, CT: Yale

University Press, 1995), 98; Edward Hickman, ed., *The Works of Jonathan Edwards*, vol. 2 (Carlisle, PA: The Banner of Truth Trust, 1974), 10.

2. George M. Marsden, *Jonathan Edwards: A Life* (New Haven, CT: Yale University Press, 2003), 220.

3. Ibid.

4. Ibid., 221.

5. Jeffery L. Sheler, "Hell Hath No Fury," *U.S. News & World Report*, January 31, 2000, 45.

6. Jon Meacham, "Is Hell Dead?" *Time*, April 25, 2011, 41–42.

7. D. A. Carson, *The Gagging of God* (Grand Rapids: Zondervan, 1996), 521.

8. See Matt. 5:22, 29, 30; 10:28; 18:9; 23:15, 33; Mark 9:43, 45, 47; Luke 12:5.

9. D. A. Carson, "Matthew," in *Matthew and Mark*, The Expositor's Bible Commentary, rev. ed., vol. 9 (Grand Rapids: Zondervan, 2010), 181–82.

10. Carson, *The Gagging of God*, 524.

11. Private correspondence with D. A. Carson, April 19, 2009.

12. Quoted in Carson, *The Gagging of God*, 520.

13. Ibid.

14. Ibid., 528.

15. R. T. France, *The Gospel of Mark*, The New International Greek Testament Commentary (Grand Rapids: Eerdmans, 2002), 382, note 70.

16. Carson, *The Gagging of God*, 533.

17. Ibid. The italics are Carson's.

18. Rob Bell, *Love Wins* (San Francisco: HarperOne, 2011), 2.

19. Ibid., 93.

20. Ibid., 81.

21. Ibid., 82.

22. Ibid., 93.

23. Carson, *The Gagging of God*, 529.

24. France, *Mark*, 383.

25. Marsden, *Jonathan Edwards*, 220–21.

26. Ibid., 221.

27. Ibid.

Chapter 5: Preaching What Jesus Says about the End Times

1. David L. Turner, *Matthew*, Baker Exegetical Commentary on the New Testament (Grand Rapids: Baker Academic, 2008), 611.

2. Darrell L. Bock, *Luke 9:51–24:53*, Baker Exegetical Commentary on the New Testament (Grand Rapids: Baker Academic, 1996), 1151.

3. Bock concludes that "it seems likely, though one cannot be dogmatic about this point, that Luke's two eschatological discourses reflect his sources' indication that there were at least two such speeches" (Ibid., 1423).

4. This outline is adapted from the analysis in Turner, *Matthew*, 565.

5. Ibid., 567.

6. This variation in Luke 12:35–38 is clearly a different parable than the one found in Matthew 25:1–13. Luke 12:35–38 concerns two men who are waiting for their master to return home from a wedding feast. Matthew 25:1–13 is a parable about ten virgins. However, the basic motif (burning lamps) and theme (watchfulness) are the same.

7. I suppose I should come clean and lay my theological cards on the table. I grew up as a classic dispensationalist (think John F. Walvoord, Charles Ryrie, etc.), but I now consider myself a progressive dispensationalist. My views are very close to those of historic premillennialism. In fact, George Ladd's *The Gospel of the Kingdom* is one of my favorite books to this day. I differ from historic premillennialism only on the timing of the rapture (I still hold to a pretribulational rapture, though I am only about 51 percent convinced!) and on the relationship between Israel and the church. While the church *replaces* Israel in covenant premillennialism, it *includes* and *extends* it in progressive dispensationalism (see David L. Turner, "Matthew and the Dispensationalists," *Journal of the Evangelical Theological Society* 53, no. 4 (December 2010): 716. Furthermore, I have much more in common with amillennialists such as Vern Poythress and Greg Beale than classical dispensationalists had in common with classical amillennialists

in the past. The divide is not what it used to be. If I am reading the landscape correctly, there is much more agreement that there is some kind of future for national Israel. The disagreement is over what exactly that future is.

8. Turner, *Matthew*, 575.

9. Ibid., 574.

10. Ibid., 587.

11. For a description of weddings in Bible times, see Philip J. King and Lawrence E. Stager, *Life in Biblical Israel* (Louisville: Westminster John Knox, 2001), 55–56.

12. Turner, *Matthew*, 598.

13. Ibid., 605.

14. See ibid. for a listing that includes Blomberg, Carson, France, Garland, Gundry, Hagner, and Keener.

15. I. Howard Marshall, *New Testament Theology* (Downers Grove, IL: InterVarsity, 2004), 110, note 34.

16. Eugene Peterson, *Reversed Thunder: The Revelation of John and the Praying Imagination* (San Francisco: HarperSanFrancisco, 1988), 9.

Chapter 6: Preaching What Jesus Says about God's Sovereignty and Human Freedom

1. This definition comes from Roger E. Olson, *Arminian Theology: Myths and Realities* (Downers Grove, IL: IVP Academic, 2006), 20.

2. See D. A. Carson, *The Gospel according to John*, The Pillar New Testament Commentary (Grand Rapids: Eerdmans, 1991), 124.

3. D. A. Carson, *The Difficult Doctrine of the Love of God* (Wheaton, IL: Crossway, 2000), 76. Mark Driscoll and Gerry Breshears argue similarly for a view they label "Unlimited Limited Atonement." See *Doctrine: What Christians Should Believe* (Wheaton, IL: Crossway, 2010), 267–70.

4. J. I. Packer, *Evangelism and the Sovereignty of God* (Downers Grove, IL: InterVarsity, 1961), 8.

5. For example, when commenting on Article 1 of the EFCA Statement of Faith, EFCA leaders say this about its conviction that God

acts with limitless knowledge and sovereign power: "Certainly, among Evangelicals there are various ways of understanding how this electing purpose of God plays out in human history, and various views, including both the Arminian/Wesleyan and Reformed versions, with their different conceptions of the mysterious interplay of the human and divine wills, are acceptable within the parameters of our EFCA Statement of Faith." *Evangelical Convictions* (Minneapolis: Free Church Publications, 2011), 46.

6. The quotations attributed to Grant Osborne, unless otherwise specified, come from a personal conversation, April 6, 2012—Good Friday!

7. Moises Silva, "The Case for Calvinistic Hermeneutics," in *Introduction to Biblical Hermeneutics*, rev. ed., ed. Walter C. Kaiser, Jr., and Moises Silva (Grand Rapids: Zondervan, 2007), 304–5.

8. Ibid., 305–7.

9. Grant R. Osborne, *The Hermeneutical Spiral: A Comprehensive Guide to Biblical Interpretation* (Downers Grove, IL: InterVarsity, 1991), 11.

10. Ibid., 15.

11. D. A. Carson, *A Call to Spiritual Reformation: Priorities from Paul and His Prayers* (Grand Rapids: Baker, 1992), 152.

12. Ibid., 153.

13. Ibid.

14. Carson says that "provided there is an honest commitment to preaching the whole counsel of God, preachers in the Reformed tradition should not hesitate for an instant to declare the love of God for a lost world, for lost individuals. The Bible's ways of speaking about the love of God are comprehensive enough not only to permit this but to mandate it." *The Difficult Doctrine*, 78.

15. D. A. Carson, *Divine Sovereignty and Human Responsibility: Biblical Perspectives in Tension*, in New Foundations Theological Library (Atlanta: John Knox Press, 1981), 220. The preface for this revised dissertation is dated July 1, 1978.

16. Ibid., 221.

Chapter 7: Preaching What Jesus Says about the Law of Moses

1. This illustration comes from Haddon W. Robinson, *The Christian Salt and Light Company: A Contemporary Study of the Sermon on the Mount* (Grand Rapids: Discovery House, 1988), 110–11.

2. Albert H. Baylis, *From Creation to the Cross: Understanding the First Half of the Bible* (Grand Rapids: Zondervan, 1996), 121.

3. A couple of centuries after Jesus, Jewish rabbis counted the individual laws and came up with 613: 248 stated positively ("You shall") and 365 stated negatively ("You shall not"). See David A. Dorsey, "The Law of Moses and the Christian: A Compromise," *Journal of the Evangelical Theological Society* 34 (1991): 321, especially note 1.

4. See chap. 9 in this volume.

5. For a helpful critique of theonomy, see William S. Barker and W. Robert Godfrey, eds., *Theonomy: A Reformed Critique* (Grand Rapids: Zondervan 1990). See also Vern Poythress, "Appendix B: Evaluating Theonomy," in *The Shadow of Christ in the Law of Moses* (Phillipsburg, NJ: P & R, 1995). Another helpful resource is Greg L. Bahnsen, Walter C. Kaiser, Jr., Douglas J. Moo, Wayne G. Strickland, and Willem A. Van Gemeren, *The Law, the Gospel, and the Modern Christian* (Grand Rapids: Zondervan, 1993). This "five views" book features one theonomist, Greg L. Bahnsen. The other four authors, varied as their views may be, are opposed to theonomy.

6. D. A. Carson, "Matthew," in *Matthew and Mark,* The Expositor's Bible Commentary, rev. ed., vol. 9 (Grand Rapids: Zondervan, 2010), 174.

7. Poythress, *The Shadow of Christ*, 265.

8. R. T. France, *The Gospel of Matthew*, The New International Commentary on the New Testament (Grand Rapids: Eerdmans, 2007), 187–88.

9. Craig L. Blomberg, *Jesus and the Gospels* (Nashville: Broadman & Holman, 1997), 249.

10. Ibid., note 42.

11. France, *Matthew*, 181.

12. Ibid.

13. Thomas R. Schreiner, *40 Questions about Christians and Biblical Law* (Grand Rapids: Kregel, 2010), 155.

14. Ibid., 157.

15. Ibid.

16. Ibid.

17. Ibid.

18. William L. Lane is correct in stating that Mark's statement "expresses the implications of Jesus' teaching, but not what he actually said at the time." *The Gospel according to Mark*, The New International Commentary on the New Testament (Grand Rapids: Eerdmans, 1974), 256. See also R. T. France, *The Gospel of Mark*, The New International Greek Testament Commentary (Grand Rapids: Eerdmans, 2002), 291–92.

19. Timothy Keller, *King's Cross* (New York: Dutton, 2011), 134.

20. Rikki E. Watts argues that "in line with ancient literary convention, Mark 1:1–3, Mark's only editorial OT citation and opening sentence, conveys the conceptual framework for this story." *Isaiah's New Exodus in Mark* (Grand Rapids: Baker Academic, 2000), 5. This conceptual framework is the long-awaited new exodus prophesied in Isaiah 40:3–5.

21. Darrell L. Bock, *Luke 9:51–24:53*, Baker Exegetical Commentary on the New Testament (Grand Rapids: Baker Academic, 1996), 35.

22. Timothy Keller, *Generous Justice: How God's Grace Makes Us Just* (New York: Dutton, 2010), 196, note 34.

23. Bock, *Luke 9:51–24:53*, 1936.

24. Schreiner, *40 Questions*, 189.

25. Gary M. Burge, *John*, The NIV Application Commentary (Grand Rapids: Zondervan, 2000), 41, 45.

26. James R. Gaines, *Evening in the Palace of Reason* (New York: Harper, 2005), 12.

27. Ibid., 237.

28. Ibid., 235.

Chapter 8: Preaching What Jesus Says about Prayer, Faith, and Miracles

1. Grant R. Osborne observes: "The form of the question with the negative particle μὴ (*mē*) expects the answer, 'Of course not!'

No parent would ever do such a capricious or cruel thing." *Matthew*, Zondervan Exegetical Commentary on the New Testament (Grand Rapids: Zondervan, 2010), 261.

2. Darrell L. Bock, *Luke 9:51–24:53*, Baker Exegetical Commentary on the New Testament (Grand Rapids: Baker Academic, 1996), 1062–63.

3. D. A. Carson, "Matthew," in *Matthew and Mark*, The Expositor's Bible Commentary, rev. ed., vol. 9 (Grand Rapids: Zondervan, 2010), 222.

4. Ibid.

5. Bock, *Luke 9:51–24:53*, 1063.

6. Caroline Lusk, "Storytelling: Laura Story Finds Blessings in the Story Gone Different," *Today's Christian Music*, May 7, 2011.

7. Carson, "Matthew," 444.

8. Osborne, *Matthew*, 657.

9. Craig L. Blomberg, *Matthew*, The New American Commentary (Nashville: Broadman, 1992), 268.

10. Ibid., 268.

11. Robert Stein, *The Method and Message of Jesus' Teachings*, rev. ed. (Louisville: Westminster John Knox, 1994), 7.

12. Ibid., 8–32.

13. Craig L. Blomberg, *The Historical Reliability of the Gospels*, 2nd ed. (Downers Grove, IL: IVP Academic, 2007), 104–5.

14. Ibid., 105.

15. Ibid., 105–7.

16. Ibid., 108–10.

17. Ibid., 111.

18. Ibid., 113–14.

19. Craig S. Keener, *Miracles: The Credibility of the New Testament Accounts* (Grand Rapids: Baker Academic, 2011), 2:761.

20. Ibid., 2:764.

21. C. S. Lewis, *The Weight of Glory: And Other Addresses* (1949; repr., San Francisco: HarperSanFrancisco, 2001), 45.

Chapter 9: Preaching What Jesus Says to the Pharisees

1. Johnny D. Guerrero, Mark Edward Mohr, and Erik Sven Sundin, "Modern Day Pharisee" is from Christafari's album, *Valley of Decision*, Gotee Records, 1996.

2. Stephen Westerholm, "Pharisees," in *Dictionary of Jesus and the Gospels*, ed. Joel B. Green, Scot McKnight, and I. Howard Marshall (Downers Grove, IL: InterVarsity, 1992), 610.

3. See Craig L. Blomberg, *Jesus and the Gospels: An Introduction and Survey* (Nashville: Broadman & Holman, 1997), 47, note 36. For a recent concise discussion of four main viewpoints in the debate over the identification of the Pharisees, see D. A. Carson, "Matthew," in *Matthew and Mark*, The Expositor's Bible Commentary, rev. ed., vol. 9 (Grand Rapids: Zondervan, 2010), 56–60.

4. See Westerholm, "Pharisees," 610. See also Gary M. Burge, Lynn H. Cohick, and Gene L. Green, *The New Testament in Antiquity: A Survey of the New Testament within Its Cultural Context* (Grand Rapids: Zondervan, 2009), 32–33, 63.

5. Burge, Cohick, and Green, *The New Testament in Antiquity*, 63.

6. Joachim Jeremias, *Jerusalem in the Time of Jesus* (Philadelphia: Fortress Press, 1969), 247.

7. Josephus, *The Antiquities of the Jews*, 17.2.42.

8. Blomberg, *Jesus and the Gospels*, 47.

9. Jacob Neusner, *The Mishnah: A New Translation* (New Haven, CT: Yale University Press, 1988), 672.

10. Oskar Skarsaune, *In the Shadow of the Temple: Jewish Influences on Early Christianity* (Downers Grove, IL: IVP Academic, 2002), 119.

11. Burge, Cohick, and Green, *The New Testament in Antiquity*, 64.

12. Skarsaune, *In the Shadow of the Temple*, 121.

13. Blomberg, *Jesus and the Gospels*, 47.

14. James C. VanderKam, *An Introduction to Early Judaism* (Grand Rapids: Eerdmans, 2001), 189.

15. Carson, "Matthew," 57.

16. Ibid., 58.

17. Burge, Cohick, and Green, *The New Testament in Antiquity*, 64.

18. Blomberg, *Jesus and the Gospels*, 48.

19. Burge, Cohick, and Green, *The New Testament in Antiquity*, 64.

20. David L. Turner, *Matthew*, Baker Exegetical Commentary on the New Testament (Grand Rapids: Baker Academic, 2008), 550.

21. Ibid.

22. I see strong irony in Jesus' description of the Pharisees as leaders to follow due to their occupation of the places of teaching authority (Matt. 23:2–3a) vis-à-vis the need for people not to follow the Pharisees due to the way they desecrate this authority (Matt. 23:3b–7).

23. See especially Turner, *Matthew*, 551. He posits that the first pair of woes concerns the way the Pharisees prevent entrance into the kingdom. The second pair focuses on how the Pharisees miss the point and cause others to miss the point when it comes to Halakhic matters—that is, rules governing everyday behavior. The third pair points out the Pharisaic problem of preoccupation with external matters while neglecting internal matters. The seventh and climactic woe charges the leaders with being the latest in a long line of those who reject and even murder the prophets.

24. Carson, "Matthew," 536.

25. R. T. France, *The Gospel of Matthew*, The New International Commentary on the New Testament (Grand Rapids: Eerdmans, 2007), 855.

26. Darrell L. Bock, *Luke 9:51–24:53*, Baker Exegetical Commentary on the New Testament (Grand Rapids: Baker Academic, 1996), 1107–8. The three reasons I cite for taking Luke 11:37–52 as an account distinct from Matthew 23:13–32 come from this discussion.

27. Ibid., 1118.

28. Ibid., 1117.

29. Jacob Neusner, *The Mishnah*, 187.

30. Ibid., 189.

31. For the view that the pronoun *their* in Deuteronomy 32:33 refers back to the enemies of Israel rather than to the Israelites themselves, see Christopher Wright, *Deuteronomy*, New International

Biblical Commentary (Peabody, MA: Hendrickson, 1996), 302; Jeffrey H. Tigay, *Deuteronomy*, JPS Torah Commentary (Philadelphia: Jewish Publication Society, 1996), 311; Peter C. Craigie, *The Book of Deuteronomy*, The New International Commentary on the Old Testament (Grand Rapids: Eerdmans, 1976), 386.

32. France, *Matthew*, 854, note 5. France notes that Davies and Allison provide "an intriguing list of roughly contemporary Jewish polemical parallels to almost all the charges leveled by Jesus" in Matthew 23 from which they conclude: "Matthew 23 is full of conventional accusations." See W. D. Davies and D. C. Allison, *A Critical and Exegetical Commentary on the Gospel according to Saint Matthew*, vol. 3, International Critical Commentary (Edinburgh: T&T Clark, 1997), 258–61.

33. Carson, "Matthew," 528–29. The quoted text in Carson's statement is a citation from David E. Garland, *The Intention of Matthew 23* (Leiden: Brill, 1979), 23–24.

34. Carson, "Matthew," 529.

35. Mark Galli, *Jesus Mean and Wild: The Unexpected Love of an Untamable God* (Grand Rapids: Baker, 2006), 75. Galli makes his statement in a discussion of Jesus' confrontation with the Pharisees in Mark 3:1–6.

36. Blomberg, *Jesus and the Gospels*, 48.

Conclusion

1. See Douglas L. Wilson, *Lincoln's Sword: The Presidency and the Power of Words* (New York: Alfred A. Knopf, 2006).

2. Philip Yancey, *The Jesus I Never Knew* (Grand Rapids: Zondervan, 1995), 129.

3. See Steven D. Mathewson, "Against Counterfeits," in *Preaching the Four Gospels with Confidence* (Peabody, MA: Hendrickson, 2013).

4. Mark Galli, *Jesus Mean and Wild: The Unexpected Love of an Untamable God* (Grand Rapids: Baker, 2006), 21.